CALL ME
A WOMAN

ON OUR WAY TO
EQUALITY AND PEACE

Praise for Call Me a Woman

"Call me a Woman: On Our Way to Equality and Peace *by Laurie Levin is one of the most fact-filled and eye-opening easy reads of our time that breaks down the reality and what we can do about it around inequality. Not only for women, this book represents equality and just being a better human being as our eyes are opened to laws, operations, beliefs and social norms that continue to keep us in the same place. The time has come for this book and it should be used in every social, educational, corporate, and governmental curriculum as reference.*"

—Anna Pereira, CEO, Soul Ventures,
Founder, The Wellness Universe

"*This book brilliantly articulates the status of gender equality in this moment, and how much of the problem is unconscious beliefs and traditions. This book is a clarion call to our hearts and minds to consciously do better. Levin provides a vision of what could be... peace, freedom, and equality. A must read for this moment.*"

—Rebecca Now, Executive Director and
Historical ReEnactor of Elizabeth Cady Stanton

"Call Me a Woman: On Our Way to Equality and Peace *is a book both long overdue and ahead of its time. Levin beautifully frames our current society, the actions and beliefs that got us here, and where we need to go to form a more perfect humanity for all of us. As a white male in the United States, I am often blinded by the inequality that faces women of every race. However, I am aware that lack of action is part of the inequality problem. Levin's book should be a discussion topic for all of us to ensure we make the change that is so crucial for the future of humanity.*"

—Martin Harvey, Founder & CEO, White Whale Web Design

"Laurie Levin's personal story of the loss of her mother at the tender age of 11 opened up a floodgate of emotions. As an oncologist, I witnessed the indescribable pain of those whose lives were shattered by losing the most important person in their lives. Women provide the love, nurturing and heart often not provided by men. Soldiers dying on the battlefield often cry out for their mom. George Floyd cried out to his mother as he was breathing his last few breaths.

Levin does a beautiful job of pointing out the inequities in the workplace and in the home. Women have made tremendous strides in all aspects of life, yet we are far from equal. In my own lifetime as a physician, I was underpaid compared to the male physicians in my department. My workload was double and even triple that of some of the men, yet when I asked for a raise, the department chief reminded me I was single and 'men have families to support.' In medical school, a surgeon told me to stand in the corner of the room and face the wall, while the male student stood at the operating room table observing and helping with the procedure. He made it clear that surgical specialties were off-limits to women, as they were too strenuous.

Thank you, Laurie Levin, for having the courage to point out the current reality of where we stand in the world today. The truth can be a source of contention for men and women alike who aspire to the notion that we belong at home raising children. Yet we can choose to have a successful and challenging career as well as give birth and raise children.

Levin's book knocks it out of the park, and I'm excited by the impact it will have to inspire the next generation and open the minds of the men in our world. Let's honor all the women in our lives because the world cannot heal without us."

—Delia Garcia, MD

"Call Me a Woman *reminds us in the very title that half of the world is still referred to as girls their ENTIRE lives. Women are diminished, belittled, not taken seriously, threatened and spend much of their lives navigating a world that is built for and by men. In order for women to succeed, especially, in the United States, they must adopt the manners, the habits of the patriarchy while diminishing their authentic selves as women. The poem preceding chapter 1 struck me in the gut. I hear the words of Sojourner Truth…'Ain't I a Woman' and the echoes of millions of women through time asking why they must be treated the way society dictates.*

Levin's book Illustrates all of the reasons why this country must make women's equality a priority, from showing how low we rate on global indexes to our lack of parental leave, childcare, healthcare and all of the measures that ensure a healthy and well-adjusted society. The 7 Habits of Equality point out very simple lessons that we can all do. Each habit forces you to look at the traditions you've labored under, the very air you breathe. It gives each woman and man a guide on how to do it differently for the next generation. Indeed, equality starts at home from the moment you are born. It is in the home that we can raise a new generation of humans who value the 'human identity' more than their identity as male or female.

I highly recommend this book and believe it's the perfect gift for high school graduates, women who are starting their careers, women who are marrying, planning a family. In other words, for every woman who wonders if she can 'have it all' and wants to know what she and the men in her life can do."

—**Lori Bunton**, Co-President, ERA-NC Alliance

"*Laurie Levin's new book,* Call Me a Woman: On Our Way to Equality and Peace, *movingly shows how traditional gender roles can cause dysfunction within families and both physical and psychological harm for women. Levin's book effectively shows how changing from traditional habits of inequality to habits of equality can help each of us as individuals and benefit society at large. This book needs to be read, heard and heeded by men as well as women!*"

—**Keith Holzmueller**, Former Vice President, Ipsos and TNS Global

"Levin's opening stories bring back memories of treatment over the years that I have brushed over. Why? It's a norm that we all have been accepting, which needs to change. Her wedding scene example is spot on. Bringing awareness to the fact that women of all ages are referred to as 'girls' hits home. I am definitely guilty of such terminology. Becoming aware is such a critical and vital step to equality and Call Me a Woman *nails it."*

—**Melinda Van Fleet**, Confidence Building Author,
Success Coach, Speaker, and Proud Woman

"In her powerful and moving book, Call Me a Woman: On Our Way to Equality and Peace, *Laurie Levin shines a spotlight on the violence and discrimination women face both nationally and internationally. Some of the statistics about equality and violence were truly shocking to me despite being an educated woman. It made me aware again how easy it is to downplay or not think about the accommodations women make, to avoid being a victim of male violence. In a deep and vulnerable manner, Levin beautifully writes of the personal life experiences that led her to write this book and that fired her passion to work for equality. This is an important book that I believe will become a reference point for business, the corporate world, and educational institutions. It is rich with data and full of hope for a new way to move toward true equality."*

—**Lorraine Langdon-Hull**, MSW, LCSW

"In her book, Call Me a Woman: On Our Way to Equality and Peace, *Laurie Levin creates a dialogue that women and men of all ages and generations can connect to. It is a sad history of how language, and even the word history, subjugates women to a less than and often forgotten role. She points out that institutionalized sexism is so prevalent that across generations and countries, past and present, women are routinely second-class citizens.*

Levin shares her own personal story of multiple rapes and experiences of male violence and institutionalized sexism, that women of all ages can relate to. Even though that was 40 years ago, college rape, date rape, and marital rape, are still unreported and judges still don't want to ruin the young men's lives, while virtually dismissing the young women's lives. Levin does a superb job of naming the sexism that has always existed against women, and offers 7 areas or places where we can develop the 'Habits of Equality.'

A must read for all teenagers, their parents, and grandparents. From the turn-of-the-century Suffragettes to Shirley Chisholm in the 1970s, to Betty Friedan and Gloria Steinem who named the female condition of being less than and oppressed, and Sapphire who spoke of the powerlessness and abuse of poor women of color, calling us to action and change in the 1960s, Laurie Levin calls all of us today, in the 21st century, to continue what is still unfinished many lifetimes later. Will inequality be our legacy or will real change happen for our daughters and their granddaughters? It is up to us! Call Me a Woman, and one day soon, in my lifetime, let me call out loud and proud, Madam President!"

—**Cathy Lebeaux**, MA, MS, LPC, BC-DMT,
Licensed Professional Counselor

"This book had me at hello. I'm referring to your opening poem. WOW! Your book pulled me in and hit such a cord that I'm sure all women will feel. I am hopeful that many men will feel the undeniable truth in this opening poem, as well.

Before I got married, I told my husband-to-be that I would be keeping my name. He tried to persuade me otherwise. So, I proposed a fair idea. I said, 'Let's flip a coin, heads we take your name, tails we take mine.' That was the end of the discussion. I kept my name. Just for a moment, though, I wanted him to consider what it felt like to give up his entire (Greek) heritage for mine (Scottish). And yet, that is what women have always done. Levin's book is one more labor pain in the birthing of a new human. This book is a ray of light!"

—**Marilyn Lyndsay**, M.Ed., BCHN

"Wow! Laurie Levin's book, Call Me a Woman: On Our Way to Equality and Peace *gives us great lessons, historical facts, and human perspectives on emotional health. One of the many things that stood out for me was the trap I think we as women fall into.*

I can look back over my 38 years of marriage and recognize my fingerprints of inequality and lack of boundaries all over it. Somewhere I lacked the ability to create boundaries and as result I found myself always carrying the load. If something negative has access to our lives, we have to ask ourselves how it got here. Honestly, it's because I allowed it and lived the habits of inequality.

Each of us can do our part with Levin's 7 Habits of Equality and apply them to our daily lives. We need to take ownership and be change agents right where we are. This book makes it so clear."

—**Thelma Scott**, Former Director of Training Non-Profit

"After reading only a few paragraphs into the book I knew I wanted to read all of it. Laurie Levin is a master storyteller and easily draws us in. Her personal account of overcoming tragedy and anti-female behavior from men in her life, penetrated my very being. This book will open our minds to the bias-enabling language that permeates our verbal discourse. Call Me a Woman *is for readers of every sex. Thank you, Laurie, for your courage and contribution to ending sexism and creating equality."*

—**Gail Zelitzky**, Founder and Business Coach

"In just the first chapter of Laurie Levin's book, Call Me A Woman: On Our Way to Equality and Peace, *I was hooked. Levin writes with such raw emotion. Her passion shines through on the pages and already has me making changes in my daily life.* Call Me A Woman *is exactly what we need right now. After reading this book, I am filled with such hope for our future. I can't wait for more people to know about and read this book!"*

—**Lauren Licciardello**, Childcare Specialist

"*In* Call Me a Woman, *Laurie Levin uses her personal journey of grief from her mother's death at a young age and subsequent abuse, including rape, to provide a guide for creating a healthier, more peaceful, and better world through equality.*

She explores and documents how positive change and better outcomes are the result of equality based on gender, race, and sexual identity in business, law, medicine, and government. Even with the progress that has been made since I entered the work world more than fifty years ago, there is still far too much that still needs to be done.

This book is a must read for parents, educators, legislators, employers, and everyone who cares about making this a better world. It is very much a story for today!"

—**Laurie Harris**, Former Senior Vice President, NFO Worldwide

"*This amazing book has opened my eyes. When my daughter became a union carpenter she came to me with weekly stories of examples of male co-worker's comments, gestures, 'pranks' (what was written on the walls of a porta-potty was disgusting and lewd) and actions. 'Boys will be boys.' Right? So, the top down (management) was promoting the hiring of women, fair and equal job assignments, equal pay, etc. But the 'rank and file' (and, of course, there are exceptions) were and are not having it. The culture is just too ingrained. And that is what must change.*

This book has opened my mind and heart to see what has been around me my whole life. And as she says in the introduction, 'Awareness is key to moving beyond any undesirable situation. We must first become aware so that we can start to ask some meaningful questions.' Not only does this book provide us with the evidence all around us pointing to the pervasive problem but points us in the direction we need to go toward a peaceful and equal world that will benefit and uplift ALL of humanity.

There has never been a more urgent time to act and this book will inspire and empower that action."

—**Pat Dulle**, BSN, RN-BC, OCN, CHTP

"Often battered and killed at the hands of men, belittled and marginalized by a global patriarchy so universally interwoven into every institution that even the well intentioned are complicit, women press forward.

Call Me a Woman: On Our Way to Equality and Peace *by Laurie Levin is not a book of grievances, although there is much to be reckoned with. Its wealth of data, statistics and anecdotes make this work a valuable source of information about gender inequality but it is not a sterile recitation of facts.* Call Me a Woman *informs and creates awareness as it inflames and indicts. Harkening to self-help books, it includes practical guidelines for achieving gender equality under the pithy label '7 Habits of Equality.' Still, it is more than a self-help work.* Call Me a Woman *is a celebration of the virtues of womanhood. Most of all, it is a resounding call for equality.*

The prevailing view is that women are in fact irrelevant. Few would dare say it but throughout the globe, this message is clear. Three women are murdered every day in America. Yet no one is protesting. 'Fifty-four percent of mass shootings between 2009 and 2018 were committed by male, intimate partners killing family members and friends,' Levin reports. Furthermore, 'In a 2018 global survey by the Thomson Reuters Foundation, the United States was named the tenth-most dangerous country in the world to be a woman,' according to Levin. Despite these and a myriad other startling statistics, this blatant terror against women is not a part of the national discourse.

Call Me a Woman *shouts out to the relevance of women. Although the work begins with Levin's personal account, it is alive with historical accounts, quotes and stories from many prominent women and men. Moreover, the ninth chapter titled, 'Voices of the Future,' features seven interviews from the younger generations in order to gain a futuristic perspective. The ugliness of gender inequality with its oppression, violence and rape is exposed, along with its pervasiveness as a global phenomenon and its entrenchment in not only the Third World, religiously dogmatic countries but also in the western developed nations.*

This work is a personal expression of author Laurie Levin's enduring struggle with gender inequality while simultaneously calling attention to the universality of the global patriarchy. Although it illustrates the horrors of violence and oppression of women, it offers solutions. It expresses hope and optimism. As its title implies, Call Me a Woman: On Our Way to Equality and Peace *is ultimately a call to action. It is a call to treat all people, particularly women, with the respect and dignity they deserve. It is a call for fairness and equality."*

—**Robert L. Brandon Jr.**, Former University Academic Support Director

"Call Me a Woman *by Laurie Levin is a book that has been needed for the last 100 years, but is especially relevant now. The United States is reeling from a long list of violent crimes against women and judicial rulings that allow their rape and murder with little or no consequences. Levin explains the situation we've gotten ourselves into with chilling statistics and examples, some painfully torn from her own experience.*

While the entire book is (sometimes frighteningly) relatable, the chapter on gender and language really struck a chord with me, perhaps because it is visible everywhere. As Laurie writes, why call a female a girl, when you can call her a woman? In the same vein, why must she be described in relation to the men in her life rather than on her own?

One of the wonderful things about this book is that Levin doesn't just preach. She offers practical courses for actions that will change our culture. In one of the later chapters of the book, she summarizes these as 'The 7 Habits of Equality.' These are *chef's kiss* perfect. If each one of us made a commitment to incorporating them into our lives, we would see change very quickly.

This book is a must read for all women (who will be able to relate to it and hear its battle cry) and men (who need to learn the lessons contained therein and get a feel for the reality women live in, which is not the same as theirs). It should be required reading in every college and university – not just in Women and Gender Studies classes, though it would certainly be at home in that setting—so that young people can see the world they are about to enter and understand what they can do to change it for the better."

—**Nicole Evelina**, Author, *Stories of Strong Women from History and Today*

CALL ME A WOMAN

ON OUR WAY TO EQUALITY AND PEACE

LAURIE LEVIN

One More Page Publishing

ISBNs:
Hardcover: 978-1-7365988-0-1
Softcover: 978-1-7365988-1-8
Kindle: 978-1-7365988-2-5
ePub: 978-1-7365988-3-2

Library of Congress Control Number: 2019914968

Book Cover by Cathi Stephenson
Interior Design by 1106Design
Cover image a derivative of work © cienpiesnf/stock.adobe.com

For Alenna,

my greatest teacher of all.
Thank you for inspiring me every day to be
a bigger thinker and better person.
Always loved you more than life,
always will.

And to all of the world's heroines,

past and present.
One day soon may you be known,
appreciated, and celebrated.

Call Me a Woman

When I turn eighteen, will you call me a woman?
If not, when I am twenty-one, thirty, or maybe fifty?
How old must I be before you call me a woman?

If I become a wife, will you call me a woman?
When I become a mother, CEO, doctor, or soldier?
Will you call me a woman then?
Who do I have to be for you to call me a woman?

You call me girl no matter my age or credentials.
And even worse: slut, slag, bitch, broad, cunt, and ho,
Just to name a few.
From trashy songs, movies, locker rooms, TV, and radio,
Money and jokes are made, and all of us pay.

Maybe you don't realize trashy names trash our lives.
Your daughters, sisters, mothers, and grandmothers alike
Misjudged, labeled, beaten, mutilated, raped, and killed
Disrespected and limited in every corner of the world.

We give ourselves away in the name of marriage,
From one man to another.
Our children are named after him,
Last names lost forever.
Sometimes entire names and identities lost when
She becomes Mrs. John Smith.
First name and family name gone.
They used to call that slavery.

Boys on the other hand are boys and then men.
Oftentimes they are referred to as gentlemen.
There doesn't seem to be any confusion when he becomes a man,
Not quite a slut, more like a stud.
Always a Mr., single or otherwise.
Oh to live with such simplicity, fairness, and respect.

If I say please and act ladylike, will you call me a woman?
I know when I get angry or become a boss, it is likely you will
Call me a bitch.
If I dress a certain way or am seen with a certain someone,
It is likely you will call me a slut.

So tell me, please.
I need to know before it's too late.
How must I act before you call me a woman?
Who must I be,
And how much longer must I wait?

—Laurie Levin

There are more months in the year than countries in the world
where women and men have equal rights.
This imbalance is the cause of the most pressing
challenges we face today.

—Laurie Levin

Contents

Introduction

I'm just a committed and even stubborn person who wants to see every child getting quality education— who wants to see women having equal rights and who wants peace in every corner of the world.

—Malala Yousafzai

Hope is not just any four-letter word, particularly amid a global pandemic, ongoing protests demanding racial equality and police reform, and a nation divided by its own history, principles, and ideals. Yet, oddly, hope is what many of us are feeling.

One of the most powerful agents of transformation is hope. Within the heart that holds it, seemingly impossible outcomes become achievable. Hope is what dreams are made of, the kind of dreams that change the world. Dr. Martin Luther King Jr. inspired us to remain hopeful, no matter what: "We must accept finite disappointment but never lose infinite hope."

Too many acts of injustice, violence, corruption, and greed have brought us to this significant time in history, here in the United States and across the globe, and we are marching and rallying together like never before. We have come to understand that inequality is encoded in a country's DNA—in its institutions, laws, language, traditions, norms, and history lessons—and plays out in every aspect of our lives. So, we march and protest for a common goal—to end the institutionalized domination of women and people of color.

By the summer of 2020, we had come to know Breonna Taylor, George Floyd, Ahmaud Arbery, Tony McDade, Mike Ramos, and Rayshard Brooks, all of whom tragically lost their lives to the ills of racism and inequality. As I learned about each of them, I was reminded of that troubling summer of 2014, when Michael Brown was shot and killed by a white police officer in Ferguson, Missouri. I lived in St. Louis at the time, not far from Ferguson. It was a difficult time for the city and nation.

The fact that this young black man had been shot multiple times by a white police officer, resulting in his death, ignited local and national outrage. We were right then, as we are now, to be outraged and deeply saddened for the lives lost, the families shattered, and communities that feel more threatened by police officers than they feel served and protected. And, sadly, six years later here we are again. Yet this time it feels different.

Reverend Al Sharpton and Congressman John Lewis shared hopeful messages after seeing hundreds of thousands of people all over the world protesting racist police practices and brutality, which far too often results in the death of a person of color. Reverend Sharpton said it feels like "a different time and season." Congressman Lewis, not long before his death in the summer of 2020, said he was moved to see people getting into what he called "good trouble."

I too felt something was different in January of 2017. I was standing among hundreds of thousands of people at the Women's March in Washington, D.C. It was one day after Donald Trump, the forty-fifth U.S. President was inaugurated, despite the fact he was seen on video by millions of voters declaring that he sexually assaults women. As I looked out into that massive crowd, I saw people of all races, genders, and ages standing with women. Perhaps finally, I thought, the country and world are paying attention.

Author Ijeoma Oluo so beautifully and boldly states in her book *So You Want to Talk About Race,* "I'm not capable of cutting away my blackness in order to support feminism that views the needs of women of color as divisive inconveniences. I'm not capable of cutting away womanhood in order to stand by black men who prey on black women. I'm a black woman, each and every minute of every day—and I need you to march for me, too."[1]

Melinda Gates challenges us in her book *The Moment of Lift: How Empowering Women Changes the World.* "Because when you lift up women, you lift up humanity. And how can we create a moment of lift in human hearts so that we all want to lift up women? Because sometimes all that's needed to lift women up is to stop pulling them down."[2]

My hope for this book is to elevate an important conversation regarding half of the world's population so that when you hear, or perhaps speak yourself, of the most important injustices of our time, the injustices women face are on that list. Most of the time when injustices are discussed—past and present, nine times out of ten (that's my personal estimate), what happens to women, no matter how egregious, rarely makes the cut. If men are not affected, the injustices are not quite unjust enough.

When we respect adult women enough to call them women, as we refer to adult men as men, and when we respect women enough to pay them and vote for them equally, then, and only then, will we have become the people who can bring peace to the world. Until then, we will always fall short. After all, women are half of every race, religion, ethnic group, economic class, and nation.

The momentum seems to be on our side, and the prize is too great to stop short. Equality and peace go hand in hand. Because when women rise, we take the world with us.

Yet, there are still many obstacles in our way. One of the most significant is the violence girls and women endure that gets so little attention. Protests and rallies do not take place for the three women murdered every day, not even the 100 women killed every month, or the 1,000 women killed every year by men in America. People aren't taking a knee and way too often not even a stand. So let's get to know some of their names because no one marched for them.

Tanisha Anderson, Yvette Smith, and Tarika Wilson . . . three African American women who died at the hands of police officers. Tanisha Anderson's family called the police for help with Tanisha, who struggled with mental illness. After being handcuffed on the ground for over twenty minutes, she was taken to the hospital, where she was pronounced dead. Yvette Smith was shot and killed by a police officer seconds after she opened the door of a friend's home. Tarika Wilson was shot and killed by a police officer while she was holding her one-year-old son.

Crimes against transgender people garner little attention, particularly transgender women of color. The years 2017 and 2018 were two of the deadliest for transgender women of color.

Viccky Gutierrez was thirty-three when she was stabbed and then her apartment was set on fire by a man she had met online. Christa Leigh Steele-Knudslien was well-known in the transgender community, both locally and nationally. Her husband confessed to Christa's murder. He stabbed and beat her to death with a hammer.

Summer of 2016. Three runners. Three tragic endings.

Karina Vetrano, thirty years old, was sexually assaulted, beaten, and murdered on her normal run in Queens, New York. Vanessa Marcotte, twenty-seven, was set on fire, her body covered in burns and discarded about a half-mile from her mother's home in Princeton, Massachusetts. Alexandra Bruger, thirty-one, was shot four times in the back on her routine ten-mile run near her home in Rose Township, Michigan.

Mass shootings are defined as shootings with four or more people killed, not including the shooter. Fifty-four percent of mass shootings between 2009 and 2018 were committed by male, intimate partners killing family members and friends.[3]

Eight of Sheena Godbolt's family members, residing in Mississippi, were shot and killed by her husband, Willie Cory Godbolt, a few weeks after she left him. Meredith Hight and eight friends were gunned down by her estranged husband, Spencer Hight, in Plano, Texas, following their divorce a few months before.

And what becomes of the perpetrators? Too often, little to nothing.

Michael Wysolovski put a girl in a dog cage for more than a year and sexually assaulted her. She was found with severe back problems, malnourishment, and ringworm. He received no jail time beyond the eight months already served in a detention center. Shane Piche, a school bus driver in upstate New York, raped a fourteen-year-old girl and got no jail time because, according to the judge, he raped only one girl. Imagine a murderer being released without jail time because they only committed one murder.

In a 2018 global survey by the Thomson Reuters Foundation, the United States was named the tenth-most dangerous country in the world to be a woman.[4] Isn't that enough to get a mention, be part of the conversation, and be included in the articles pertaining to the most important injustices of our time? And why isn't it enough for our U.S. elected officials to renew the Violence Against Women Act? Why must so many women continue to die so that known domestic abusers can keep their guns?

Some of the other deadliest places in the world to be female are in Latin America and the Caribbean. Honduras, El Salvador, and Guatemala have some of the highest homicide rates for women in the world. The Trump administration attempted to keep women and families from entering the country because of gender-based violence while allowing entry to those fleeing violence due to race, religion, political affiliation, or social group membership.

After living more than six decades, it is devastating at times to still feel the stunning difference there is in the way females are considered and treated throughout the world. Optimism has always led me to believe we are at least moving in the right direction and away from the double standards that exist about every place females live and work—and the epidemic rates of violence against females.

However, here we are in the United States—a nation that elected a president after he told us, in some detail, how he assaults women. This sadly was followed by people making light of it, declaring it "locker room" talk.

We do not commonly hear people publicly excuse racist or anti-Semitic remarks because it's "locker room" banter. This is because racist and anti-Semitic speech is not considered okay in a locker room or otherwise. Yet, this fails to hold true for women. By excusing, diminishing, mislabeling, and joking about hate speech, in any shape or form, we fail to see how the trivialization of violence against women not only perpetuates violence, but it also reflects our broader view of women and their place in the world.

I am pretty confident in saying a female version of Donald Trump, captured on video declaring she sexually assaults people, and grabs them by the _____, would have been unelectable. I am also pretty confident in saying a female version of Donald Trump would not have been electable, regardless of the offensive comments we heard on the campaign trail and during his presidency. This is an example of the gap, the differential treatment, the starkly different double standards created by institutionalized sexism. One group, over and over again, gets a pass; they are routinely allowed, accepted, or acknowledged (aka entitled) while another group is routinely denied, dismissed, denigrated, (aka oppressed), or worse.

The countless numbers of oppressed individuals lost over time, who have been more qualified than entitled ones to lead, invent, and create, hurt us all. The loss of potential and promise is too staggering to comprehend, yet current-day circumstances and events remind us we must do better.

Awareness is key to moving beyond any undesirable situation. We must first become aware so that we can start to ask some meaningful questions.

- ▸ Why do national protests and nonstop media attention, month after month, follow a police shooting when the victim is male and rarely when the victim is female?

- ▸ Why do so few rapists ever see a day in jail?

- ▸ Why do most mass shootings involving a man killing his family not get the same attention as a man killing people on the job, in a bar, or at a concert?

- ▸ Why are so many boys and men harassing, assaulting, raping, and killing children, women, and men? Perhaps this is the most important question of all.

Because we live in patriarchal cultures permeating every race, economic class, nationality, and religion, we see women treated this way universally. Instead of labeling it what it is—male supremacy and sexism, which like white supremacy and racism are oftentimes fatal—we call this "ism" tradition, old school, or "to be expected," as the forty-fifth president of the United States said about rape in the military. Furthermore, these crimes oftentimes get lumped into "crimes of passion" with sub-headings like date rape and domestic violence, avoiding naming the perpetrators altogether.

We tell women what to do to reduce their risk of becoming a victim instead of focusing on men reducing violence. And when we do address sexual harassment and assault, that's when we seem to hear from men the most. "Well, I'm not violent. I've never raped anyone."

The majority of men are not violent. However, in a country ranked the tenth most dangerous in the world to be female, too many men in the United States clearly are. It would be far more helpful if we heard from men about their concerns for the epidemic rates of violence against girls and women rather than their discomfort when male violence comes up.

Of course, women can also be violent. However, it is important to remember that women are police officers, scorned spouses, and disgruntled employees, yet for the vast majority of police shootings, mass shootings, neighborhood shootings, and disgruntled employee shootings, women are not the shooters—men are.

Imagine if male violence was reduced to the level of female violence in the world. Imagine not reading about violence in the news every day. Imagine how much safer the world and our lives would be. Imagine how differently a woman's life would be if she didn't have to live in fear about a walk home, or to her car, or to the subway, or if the car breaks down, or living on a college campus, or on a first date.

So we must look to see why we continue to support the heightened significance and domination of men as their right and the insignificance and subordination of women as their role, all of which lead to staggering rates of violence, discrimination, and poverty. Women go about their lives being paid less, living fearfully about the violence that may occur on campus, around the next corner, or in their own homes; less apt to be elected to office; less likely to get the job or the promotion; less likely to be celebrated in history, and on and on.

Equality can become our reality when each of us comes to terms with how we uphold inequality. The long-standing domination of men over women is reflected in our language, traditions, choices, votes, and what we do and don't pay attention to.

In the nineteenth century, women's rights leader and suffragist Elizabeth Cady Stanton said, "The prolonged slavery of women is the darkest page of history."

In the twenty-first century, former President Jimmy Carter said, "The abuse of women and girls is the most pervasive and unaddressed human rights violation on the earth."[5]

There are more than 100 years between these two quotes, and experts tell us gender equality will not be achieved for another 100 years!

The good news is that cultures and nations are made up of people and people change the world all the time.

> *Sometimes the heart sees what is invisible to the eye.*
> **—H. Jackson Browne Jr.**

I believe it is our hearts we must call upon now and act accordingly.

We are living in the most precarious of times with growing uncertainty about what the future will bring. It is becoming quite clear, as we navigate our way through the Covid-19 health crisis, along with rampant human rights injustices that plague societies around the world, that our lives are inextricably linked and that we need one another—in good health, in good schools, with fair pay, fair policies, and fair systems, to survive and to survive well.

My ultimate hope, as you read this book, is for your heart and mind to open wide with each page turned and that you see a new, more loving, fair, and caring way forward. We need all hands on deck right now to

xxxiv   CALL ME A WOMAN

unleash the extraordinary potential humanity brings to the planet to solve our greatest challenges.

Call Me a Woman: On Our Way to Equality and Peace is an opportunity for each of us to take an honest look at our own lives, the language we use, the choices we make, and the traditions we pass along to see where we contribute to the inequality that girls and women face throughout the world.

And to this, I must add one additional and very important point.

When one group is treated unequally, the dominating group lives with privileges at the expense of those they dominate. Whereas men have advantages in life because of gender inequality, there is no question it comes at a great cost to them as well.

Gender-based expectations are harmful to us all, regardless of race, nationality, religion, or sexual orientation. They put undue pressure on people to take on roles they would not otherwise have chosen or perhaps live a whole lifetime without full expression of their true selves and desires.

As we engage in this conversation to expand our levels of awareness, understanding, commitment, and compassion, we will transform our fears of moving beyond that which has been to all that can be.

We will finally treat each other the way we want to be treated ourselves.

Fair and square.

Equal.

Part One

The Unfinished Business
of Our Time

*Progress is impossible without change, and
those who cannot change their minds
cannot change anything.*

—George Bernard Shaw

ONE

Life's Hard Knocks

*All truth passes through three stages. First, it
is ridiculed. Second, it is violently opposed.
Third, it is accepted as being self-evident.*

—Arthur Schopenhauer

Many of us can look back at a single moment in our lives, when
our world turned upside down, and life as we knew it was gone forever.
That moment came for me when my father sat us kids on the edge of
his bed and told us our mother was dying.

"All we can do is pray," he said.

We weren't really a praying family, so I had no idea what he was
talking about, nor did I have any idea my mother was that sick. How
could stomachaches end her life and how would we ever manage without
her? There are simply no words to express the confusion and the pain I
felt, some of which remains today.

My mother, Mildred Burgess Levin, was thirty-nine years old when she passed away in 1967. I was eleven, my brother Mark sixteen, and my sisters, Cindy and Cathy, thirteen and eight. I would come to understand that at this age, I was old enough to feel the loss but too young to know how to deal with it.

The day of her funeral was the first day I had been outside in some time. As I walked toward the black limousine parked at the edge of the driveway—an unbearable walk that seemed a mile long—I started to notice something was different. At first, I couldn't figure out what it was. Not long before, I undoubtedly played with friends in the neighborhood, not noticing how blue the sky was, the color of the grass, or the street signs.

Walking toward the limousine, it finally occurred to me. The colorful world I experienced and took for granted was gone. The grass was the first thing I noticed, then the street signs that used to be red and yellow. Now I saw only shades of gray. My heart was broken, and all I felt was deep despair. The loss seemed too great to bear. I now lived in a colorless world and in a whole lot of pain.

I can't remember exactly how long my colorless world lasted. The months and childhood that followed are like a kaleidoscope, without all the colors, just bits and pieces of memories held together by string. I simply could not imagine being in the world without my mother and knew her death would leave an unfillable hole in my heart and my life.

She made everything work for our family, no matter what was going on in our lives. We could always count on her, which created a wonderful sense of security. Her love and support allowed us to be our best and to do the things we were passionate about. For me, that was dance and art.

The kitchen table was oftentimes cleared to make way for my art supplies, which my mother always made sure I had. And every week off to dance classes she and I would go.

I attended dance classes at a studio in University City, a St. Louis suburb not far from where I lived. One of my favorite memories is my mother on the other side of the glass partition, her eyes fastened on me as I danced. She looked so happy and proud. Dancing was a true passion of mine, and when I think back to that time in my life, her being part of it was the best part of all.

Together, my parents created a loving home. My dad's masculine strivings were balanced by my mother's generous and nurturing parenting. By the time we woke up in the morning, she would have breakfast and lunches made. When we came home from school, she was always there with a snack. Then out the door we'd go to hang out with friends until dinner. Then it was all about homework and family time watching a favorite TV show. She cared for our family, our home, and in between all that, she somehow found the time to support the family business.

My father loved and cared for us deeply as well. He was a wonderful and sweet man, yet there was a disconnect with his heart when it came to how he prioritized his time and shared himself with his children. He, too, was devastated by the loss of his wife and mother of his four children. He loved her very much, yet I don't remember him ever talking about my mother again after she passed away, unless prompted by a family member or friend. I don't think it was that he didn't want to. It was more that he wasn't able. So we marched on like little soldiers, denying the pain we were all experiencing.

We watched him go right back to work after the funeral, ten-plus hours a day in the family shoe business most days of the week. "Go back to what you were doing before and keep doing it" seemed to be the message. There was no time to grieve the loss of friends on the front lines or wife and mother of your children. I suppose he felt this was the best way to protect us and move on with our lives. As I learned with time, this couldn't have been further from the truth.

When my mother died, my dance classes ended, and my art table disappeared. I don't remember my father ever mentioning either. Was it not important to him? Had he ever noticed my artwork or thought about my love for dance? In reality, I don't think he had.

He was clearly a product of his time, as my mother was of hers. Like so many men of his era, he was raised to provide material well-being at the expense of his nurturing side. We needed and missed that part of him as we worked to put our lives back together and move forward without our mother. We were fortunate to have a large family, filled with loving grandmothers, aunts, uncles, and cousins. They helped in so many ways to fill the gaps.

In my mother's absence, I came to notice in time the feel of the house had changed. The extraordinary gift of her presence, her love, and her support were gone forever. Traditional masculine values became the household norm. A lot fewer words—get the job done, and don't talk too much about your feelings.

I also felt like an outsider without her as my interests were different from everyone else in the family. Sports and math were big deals and what oftentimes brought us together. So, I made up my mind. To feel part of the new team, it wasn't going to happen the old way, with the old me. I let art and dance go and moved on, focusing on sports, making the school teams, and my math classes.

Another defining moment for me came on a Sunday afternoon when my father and us kids were in the carport working to get the lawn mower fixed. Someone said something, and I started to cry. I don't remember what was said or who said it, but I remember my father said something like, "Laurie, don't be a crybaby." I felt embarrassed, and it became clear to me at that very moment that crying was not okay and that I had better toughen up.

It was in my teen years when I started putting things together. My life inside my home began to match up with what I was experiencing out in the world. Those same traditionally masculine-defined values were clearly more valued; anything else was considered weak. Emotions should be shared sparingly, and boys were more highly considered and celebrated than girls.

Double standards were all around me. At school, the cheerleaders attended the boys' sporting events but not the girls' events. The boys had an amazing gym at my high school back in the 1970s, like an NBA basketball court with glass backboards and beautiful stands that seated hundreds. The girls' gym was upstairs and so small that the few spectators it could hold had to stand around the perimeter of the gym with their backs against the wall, constantly dodging both the ball and players.

It was men who were our principals and heads of the districts. It was men we read about in history books. With the exception of the Salem witches, I don't recall learning much of anything about women in history classes or any class for that matter. Certainly nowhere near the time was spent on the women's rights movement and its leaders as was spent learning about the civil rights movement and its leaders.

Given the constant cues and messages that being female was lesser, resentment and angst became my frequent companions. By the time college was in my future, I felt a change was needed. So I decided to go far away, to another country, in fact. I think I was hoping to erase the heartache and disappointments, move on, make new friends, and get a fresh start.

At orientation during my first week of college in Puebla, Mexico, the women were given whistles in the event we were attacked on campus. I remember throwing my whistle into a drawer, never thinking about it again—until it was too late.

He was a friend of a friend, one of the stars of the basketball team, someone I thought I could trust to walk back to the dorm with after a fun night out dancing. That proved not to be the case.

When we reached my dorm, I said goodbye, and as I was turning toward my building, he yanked me backward so hard that I couldn't get myself upright from that point on. There were no words, no cries for help. I couldn't budge. He must have weighed twice as much as me and then some. It felt like a ton of bricks had dropped from the sky, and I was under them. That feeling of helplessness, the lack of control I had over my body and my life, is something I've never been able to completely shake from my memory.

It would take me thirty years before I talked about being raped that first year of college, partly I suppose because I had been taught to handle trauma in a certain way. Don't talk about it, and maybe the whole thing will go away, as though it never happened. Of course, it never does go away.

There were so many conflicting feelings for me at the time of the rape—anger, and perhaps rage, that women were given whistles rather than addressing men's criminal behavior, anger at what he did to me, and what he thought he had the right to do. At the same time, I was scared. He must have been wondering what I was going to say and do. I was wondering myself. I was filled with uncertainty during the days and weeks that followed as I walked from class to class, on the same campus he walked every day, and where he continued to play basketball, most likely to cheers and adulation. I wouldn't know. I didn't attend any more games at the university.

I wanted very much to have a normal college experience. After all, these are supposed to be some of the best years of your life. Aren't we told that before heading off for college? I knew if I said anything, my college experience would be anything but that.

So I chose to say nothing. It would be my word against his. I was in another country, and he was a star athlete. I had come to learn, as many of us have, that drinking in a bar for females was a whole different ball game than what our male counterparts experienced. The guys could wear whatever they wanted, drink, and still be deemed credible. Once again, I toughened up, so I thought, and erased the memory. So I thought.

I left the university the next semester, moved to Mexico City, and taught English in Zona Rosa to corporate executives from around the world. One night after work, as I walked to my apartment from the subway station, a young man jumped out of nowhere from behind, bringing me to my knees on the sidewalk. He grabbed my bag. Given the important documents I often had with me, I fought him and held on tight. He ended up with a paper bag full of crumbs from a snack I had eaten after work. I was beginning to learn to fight back.

During my college years, I was to have several more instances of men thinking they were entitled to help themselves to my body. One put his hand down my shirt on a subway, where we were packed shoulder to shoulder, and grabbed my breast. I never hit anyone before that moment, nor afterward; however, my instincts, or maybe it was rage, kicked in, and my fist found itself in his face within seconds. With all eyes on him at that moment, he ran off the subway at the next stop. Another time while out shopping with friends, a man behind us put his hand up my shorts and grabbed me.

I remember thinking at the time, "What is up with the men of the world? Have they no control of themselves? What is it they don't get? What have they learned about themselves and females that they treat us this way? Do they not think about their daughters, sisters, or mothers because this is their lives too?"

Laura Bates, from the UK, addresses how this has become normalized in many cultures because so many women endure harassment and assault. In her 2016 book *Everyday Sexism*, women share their stories of sexism, street harassment, discrimination on the job, sexual assault, and rape. Bates tells us, "Women are silenced by both the invisibility and the acceptability of the problem."[1]

Unfortunately, the assaults didn't end when I came back to the States. In fact, they got worse. I came back to St. Louis to complete my undergraduate degree and MBA. I worked full time during the day and went to school at night.

I never parked my car in the university garage, regardless of how far I had to walk. Being in a dark or a tight space sends chills up my spine still today. Instead, I parked in the single parking spaces that wrapped around the campus because they were well lit with streetlamps. No matter how much farther I had to park in rain or snow, no matter how late I would be for class, I didn't use garage parking throughout the many years it took to complete both undergraduate and graduate school. To this day, I sometimes find myself driving around in circles looking for a parking space on the street, passing one garage after another.

One summer, needing a break from work and school, I took a road trip to see a girlfriend who had moved from St. Louis to Atlanta. We planned a trip to Myrtle Beach for a long weekend, and I was heading to pick her up. It was in the mountains of Tennessee that once again I felt that combination of intense fear and anger.

I was driving my brand-new, little blue Honda Civic. I was excited to be traveling on my own, in my first new car, and hanging out on the beach for a few days with a good friend I hadn't seen in some time. I noticed a truck coming up behind me closely and then backing off. The driver continued to do this for many miles. Then he passed me and made all kinds of sexual gestures with his tongue. I can picture him still today, and my stomach turns.

He slowed down when he was in front of me and raced toward me when he was behind. This continued for a while, with no other cars in sight. I became extremely frightened driving on mountainous roads, in a small car, with an unhinged man following me in a semi-truck.

I was finally able to get ahead of him and stay there, heart pounding, and looking back for miles, afraid he would reappear. Years later, watching the movie *Thelma and Louise*, I cheered as the co-stars set their harassing truck driver's truck on fire. I think many other women did as well.

Then in my mid-twenties, I was in a bad relationship with a man who couldn't control himself when he was angry. He blackened my eyes, pushed me down, and stomped on my back. There were a couple of occasions when I looked up in my rearview mirror, out for lunch breaks, and I saw him following me. My self-worth was high enough to know I wasn't going to put up with that, and I left. Unfortunately, before I was able to move out of our shared apartment, he raped me. This time, I called him a rapist; I said it out loud. His reply to me? "You can't rape a woman you live with."

Sometime later in my own apartment, living fearfully still, I was awakened one night, around midnight, to a loud pounding noise. There was a party going on in an apartment close by, so I didn't think much about it and closed my eyes to go back to sleep. I heard it again and realized the pounding was at my door.

I walked into the hallway shaking, my heart beating as loud as the banging. My eyes were glued to that door. I saw it open and a hand attempting to slide the chain loose—his hand. I knew I was in trouble—serious trouble.

My response was immediate. With everything I had, I ran toward the door and threw my whole body at it, slamming it as hard as I possibly could. Lucky for him, he moved his hand out of the doorway in time. With great effort, I was able to talk him down from his anger over my leaving. I'll never forget him saying he didn't understand why I was so angry; after all, he hadn't killed anybody in my family. Was that a threat, I wondered, or did he believe what he had done to me was not criminal enough?

I took the next several years to focus on my career. I was all in. I was enjoying life again, earning promotions at work, and traveling as much as I could. My brother had moved to San Francisco, and it became my favorite city.

I was working more than sixty hours a week, so vacations were highly anticipated. One summer I was excited about taking some time off and heading west to San Francisco for a few days. After a beautiful day of sightseeing, I had some time to kill before my brother and I were meeting for dinner. So I decided to hang out for a bit, outside his place, enjoying the city and a little people watching.

Suddenly a large man jumped out of his car and began pulling me into it. I held onto a streetlamp for dear life, so scared as I fought to keep myself from being dragged into his car. All of a sudden he let go. I have no idea why. Maybe he saw a police car approaching. All I do know is if he had succeeded, I probably would not be here today.

I experienced a similar scenario several years later. I was power walking in Oak Park, Illinois, visiting my sister with my daughter, who was probably eight or nine years old at the time. It was about 6:30 a.m., and I was excited to be up and out on a beautiful morning.

I saw a man in a red jeep make an abrupt turn down the street ahead of me. He jumped out and stood behind his car, looking at me around the corner of his jeep and then quickly pulling his head back so I wouldn't see him. My heart raced, and I knew if I continued to walk down that next block, I could be pulled into his car. He was a big guy, and I knew I wouldn't stand much of a chance.

I turned around quite slowly to make it appear as though it was where I was headed all along and walked down the middle of the street for greater visibility. I remember thinking, "You are not going to take my daughter's mother from her. No way, no how." Nothing had been harder for me than growing up without my mother, and that was not going to happen to my daughter. I turned my head slightly to see if he was following me and saw him jump back in his jeep and drive away on screeching tires.

Later that day, I shared with my daughter what might have happened had I continued to walk down the street toward the man, so she would learn what to do if she felt impending danger. I had heard women can be so concerned about appearing discourteous that they walk themselves right into danger. I couldn't bear that any one of the things that had happened to me could happen to her.

My anger hit a peak at this point in my life as I felt my world getting smaller, now even fearful in broad daylight power walking. I can count at least six more occasions when I was in extreme danger from male violence. As a result, fear was creeping into everyday life, everyday decisions. Parking in garages made my heart race, as did walking down sidewalks with men sitting in their cars, even more so if they were standing alongside them.

It didn't seem fair. I felt so little attention was given to female victims and male perpetrators. Here I was in my early thirties, and I had been raped more than once, beaten, stalked, mugged, groped, almost abducted, and terrorized.

Some have asked me why I think this has happened to me. I think the better, fairer question is why so many boys and men are doing this to girls and women and why they feel so horribly entitled to act this way and expect little or no consequences.

I have felt internal conflict for decades, and still do, over the part I have played in the "little or no consequences" that allowed my perpetrators to not find themselves charged and convicted of a crime. I think back to my college years and what might have happened had I sought justice for the rape I experienced on campus and then in my early twenties when I was beaten, raped, and stalked. I'll never know of course. What I do know is it is one of the reasons I wrote this book. It is my way of turning all of it into something positive—making a positive difference, I hope, albeit four decades later.

I'm not sure if it was a lack of courage that held me back from seeking justice or our "boys will be boys" culture that has us almost believing that bullying, assaulting, fighting, and raping are all more attributable to nature than criminal behavior. This same "boys will be boys" culture leaves countless victims along the way who feel no matter what they have endured, he will walk away unscathed, while you will go through hell all over again. I suspect, for me, it was a bit of both.

In my search for peace over the years, I have gone from anger and resentment to sadness and back again, many times, wondering if we will ever live in a safe, equitable, and peaceful world. Are we capable?

One day my mother was there, and love, kindness, and compassion prevailed in our home and my world. After her death, work, achievement, and money took priority and seemed to be the way of the world.

So where do we even begin to sort all this out and live together fairly, responsibly, and peacefully?

As Gandhi said, "We must be the change we want to see in the world." Assuming this to be true, who we hold ourselves to be is the place to start.

TWO

The Place to Begin

*When we can no longer change a situation, we are
challenged to change ourselves.*

—**Viktor Frankl**

Because of the vastness of the challenges we face all around the
world, what is needed most is a change at our very core. It is from this
place—how each of us defines ourselves and our place in the world—that
we make all of our decisions.

For most of us, one aspect of our identity has been defined for us
within a binary human construct called gender. When I was growing
up, you checked one of two boxes: girl or boy, end of story. By doing
so, child rearing, expectations, rules, traditions, and opportunities were
set in motion. Today we're breaking that wide open, and people are
courageously expressing gender on their terms rather than what was
ascribed at birth. Parents are parenting with more awareness of the

gender-based messages their children receive, from inside and outside the home, that can ultimately limit their child's expectations of themselves and of others.

With more than fifty gender options on Facebook today, I will leave room for those much more qualified than I to speak about them. I continue to learn from resources like Sam Killermann, author and social justice comedian, who wrote *A Guide to Gender: A Social Justice Advocate's Handbook.* His website, www.itspronouncedmetrosexual.com, is dedicated to educating people about gender identities, gender expression, sexuality, and social justice.[1] The website is filled to the brim with articles, edugraphics, videos, workshops, and activities that provide a great way to learn and understand that there are many gender identities people are identifying with and ways to express them.

I also reach out to young people and learn from them how to use more inclusive, nongender-specific language, and pronouns that reflect inclusion and equality, which have always been important for a fair and just society. I know I won't get it 100 percent right in this book, so please forgive me when I fail to represent a deeper understanding. I am a work in progress.

Kimberlé Crenshaw, a professor at Columbia University in New York as well as UCLA, coined an important term in 1989 to describe the different ways individuals experience discrimination. She called it intersectionality. Audre Lorde, poet, feminist, and civil rights activist, said there isn't a "single-issue struggle" because we do not live "single-issue lives."

We have a gender, a way we express gender, sexual orientation, race, possibly religion, and nationality. We have physical abilities that vary and overlap each of these, as we do an economic class. As a white Jewish cisgender female, I have experienced discrimination and violence due to my religion and gender but not my sexual orientation or race. All experiences and stories are pertinent, must be considered, and included to create compassionate and meaningful solutions to our most pressing challenges.

To continue to learn and deepen my own understanding, I met with a group of women for several months in 2019. I was the only Caucasian in the group. We shared stories and perspectives. Mostly I listened, and I always left struck by both the similarities in our lives and the stark differences. I am also reading articles and books written by female feminists of color. Their pain and struggles need to be understood, shared, and cared about. Far too many conversations, movements, and policy discussions have occurred without them. Only when we deepen this understanding can we begin to chip away at the institutions and policies that disproportionately affect women and people of color and harm, limit, and lessen lives.

At social and business meetings, I always look around the room to see how diverse the group is. If they all look like me, I bring that into the conversation and challenge myself and the group to bring greater diversity to future gatherings.

As we look in new directions to create greater diversity, fairness, and equality, it is important to remember that in every time and place, a culture appears normal to a significant portion of the population, particularly those who hold power. For example, in 1963, Betty Friedan challenged what we called "normal" with her groundbreaking and controversial book, *The Feminine Mystique*.[2] The "mystique" Friedan spoke of was the limited belief held by most that women belonged in the home and were defined by their husbands and children.

African American women and other working-class women had been working outside of the home for decades prior to Friedan's book, and therefore many felt the book was not relevant to their lives. Yet the belief that women, whether they work outside of the home or not, were most responsible for home and children, has been hard to shake off—then and now. The companion mystique was that men's identity was to be found almost entirely in their economic success, sexual conquests, and athletic ability—equally as hard to shake.

It is now more than half a century since *The Feminine Mystique* was published. When I first revisited these traditionally gender-defined identities several years ago, I thought they were outdated. And then I stopped and thought, well, maybe not.

There is no question that women today have many more options than our mothers and grandmothers had. Women have children, or not, run businesses, are leaders in government, and by and large, these choices are respected by both women and men.

Are there still remnants of the old feminine mystique Friedan described? Yes. Are women today defined entirely by men and children? Not so much.

The comparable masculine mystique doesn't seem to have changed nearly as much. Some change, yet the male identity is still largely based on power in the areas of money, sex, and athletics, which is as limiting as the feminine mystique was for women. These arenas alone are simply not meaningful pursuits, as Frank Pittman, author of *Man Enough*, points out.

According to Pittman, "Men fight for turf and wrestle for control over people and things, whether through war, armed robbery, or corporate takeovers. They are trying to feel like men but no matter what they do, they never seem to feel man enough. Masculinity is an artificial state, a prize to be won by fierce struggle."[3]

Coach Joe Ehrmann, a former NFL star, high school football coach, and inspirational speaker would agree. He fervently feels the problems we face today are a result of our sons being raised without an important human dimension. Boys are not raised to understand their feelings, says Ehrmann, and "if you don't understand your feelings then you won't be able to understand love—critical for having empathy."[4]

Which brings us to a discussion of an oftentimes dangerous concept called emasculation. First, I have never heard of a woman being "defeminized." I'm not even sure what that would entail. Yet, it's not uncommon to hear heterosexual men and women claim a man has been emasculated, most commonly by a woman's behavior, or her success, or her desires, or her talents.

When an external force can emasculate (or defeminize) someone, that person's sense of self is based on a flimsy and false sense of reality. As Pittman states, the male identity is based on men "wrestling for control of people and things." By definition, the burden of a heterosexual man's sense of self largely falls on the backs of women.

As long as he has the bigger job, makes more money, is the one to propose, gets the family name, pays for the dinner, leads in dancing, and is her boss, then he retains his manhood; in other words, as long as she doesn't retain her sanity and achieve her full potential.

This notion of emasculation reminds us of what we oftentimes hear following a rape: What was she wearing? What was she drinking? Why did she stay with him so long? These are all ways to control and wield power without accountability.

It's male supremacy and misogyny on steroids. It's ridiculous. It's archaic. It's dangerous. And for many of us, we've been on the other side of a fist because of it.

The gender gap will close and equality will be achieved when "being a man" does not require the domination of others and the pursuit of power. We are all liberated as we move closer to equality and further away from patriarchal machinations like emasculation.

What I am convinced of is that for a society to be truly great, two things must occur. Regardless of how a person identifies and expresses themselves, as it relates to gender, an all-inclusive human identity, one that allows for the entire spectrum of human emotions such as love, compassion, and kindness, is a must. Imagine if each of us identified with that first and foremost.

Second, each of us must embrace our rightful place as equal partners in the world, regardless of our demographics. Nothing less, nothing more.

Until this occurs, we will continue to see the problems of today—corporate greed, economic and environmental disasters, violence, war, and poverty—continue and worsen. As each of us has a tremendous stake in this; we must each look to see where we play a part.

Back in the post-Friedan, "women's liberation" era, parents consciously raised their daughters differently. Little girls were given a wider variety of toys to play with including bats and balls and science kits, along with dolls and arts and crafts. Pretty in pink was on its way out. Daughters were encouraged to dream of being anything they wanted.

And yet those same parents continued to raise sons traditionally for fear they would not be able to take their place in society. The sight of their little boy not participating in sports or being "one of the guys," preferring a doll to a truck, still today makes even enlightened parents uneasy. As Gloria Steinem once said, "We've begun to raise daughters more like sons, but few have the courage to raise our sons more like our daughters."[5]

This is why the feminine mystique of the 1960s is much less prevalent than the male mystique today. Parents transformed the lives of their daughters, while keeping their son's lives limited and unfulfilling in a world that no longer needed a lion slayer or sole breadwinner.

So how do we raise our children differently? And will it work?

It worked for Joe Ehrmann. As a football coach, his Baltimore high school team's training was a kind of Men 101 course. He focused on teaching these young men about relationships, the responsibilities they had to one another, and how to make relationships work through challenges that come on and off the field.

"Masculinity, first and foremost, ought to be defined in terms of the capacity to love and be loved," Ehrmann says. He further explains, "Emotional illiteracy, superiority over women, and violence are not inherent to masculinity. They are the result of how we socialize boys into men."[6]

It's worth noting that Ehrmann's team was undefeated three out of six seasons, also achieving the number one ranking in Baltimore in

2002, number one ranking in Maryland, and number fourteen ranking nationally in his eight years coaching this Baltimore high school team. In other words, winning (on or off the field) doesn't have to come at the expense of a person's humanity.

The distinct traits that we label masculinity and femininity lie within each of us. No gender or group of people of any kind holds a monopoly on love, kindness, compassion, courage, and self-assuredness. When someone is in need, compassion and empathy are needed, and when we want to get something done, self-assuredness and courage move us forward. Human beings need to be capable of all of this, and they can be when raised and socialized accordingly.

Just as we've taught our daughters to be relationship savvy, we can do the same for our sons. We can teach our sons to feel and express their emotions and positively acknowledge them when they do so. We can share the importance of quality relationships, modeling them, no longer limiting the expression of love, care, and compassion to females and no longer defining and limiting boys to athletic abilities, aggressiveness, and domination. No longer can half the world's population be limited to power-seeking pursuits. And we must respect and honor boys and men who respect and care for others.

We must also teach them to respect and honor women. We can tell them clearly that when they—or musicians, journalists, athletes, or celebrities—call adult women girls, slut, ho, cunt, or bitch, women are denigrated and dismissed. When they allow those names to be used without objection, they are also culpable when their daughters, mothers, sisters, and grandmothers are denigrated, dismissed, or worse.

At the same time, women must choose new options that do not reinforce gender-based double standards and the status quo. Although opportunities have certainly increased for women, many of our most important choices are no different than the choices our mothers and grandmothers made.

Most women give up their last name in marriage, take their husband's name, and pass it along to their children, after a marriage ceremony where she is "given away" from father to husband, while her mother sits to the side and watches. We still refer to women as "girls" when these women are well beyond childhood. For the most part, women do not call it "work" when they work at home taking care of home and children, and far too often, women can be heard calling other women derogatory names and diminishing them as they seek leadership roles.

As these practices and choices are part of the same culture that has brought about tremendous changes for women, they seem normal, yet they are no different than the limiting aspects of the feminine mystique we have been dismantling over the past five decades.

As we move beyond the limiting gender-based norms of our time, the masculine identity as we know it today will cease being that artificial prize Dr. Pittman described. Women, their work, their bodies, and lives will be valued and respected. Men, their kindness, compassion, and empathy will become measures of success and strength. Then we will become the people who expect less of another based on gender and more from ourselves based on our ability to love, care, and share.

And before too long, we will be heartened, instead of disheartened, by the news of the day as we live in a world where love, care, and compassion become the dominant forces of our lives.

THREE

A Lesson from History

No country can ever truly flourish if it stifles
the potential of its women and deprives itself of
the contributions of half of its citizens.

—Michelle Obama

In every time and place, different and unequal standards we hold as truths can appear normal even to those who stand for equality and change. For many, knowing what to expect can seem less threatening than not knowing. In many countries, challenging the status quo is a matter of life and death.

In 1774, John Adams was one of five men writing the Declaration of Independence. Adams was a man who prided himself on being fair, an intellect, and a champion for independence. Yet it took his wife, Abigail Adams, holding down the farm and family in Massachusetts, to remind her husband, "Remember the ladies."

That quote, "remember the ladies," is famous, but the rest of Abigail Adams's passage in her well-preserved letter to her husband in 1776 is eye-opening:

Be more generous and favorable to [the ladies] than your ancestors. Do not put such unlimited power into the hands of the Husbands. Remember all men would be tyrants if they could. If particular care and attention is not paid to the Ladies we are determined to foment a rebellion, and will not hold ourselves bound by any Laws in which we have no voice, or representation.[1]

These are truly amazing words written in a time when women had virtually no rights. Women were not allowed into higher education. They could not vote or hold office. They were not allowed professional occupations. Maid, cook, governess, and laundress, all low-paying jobs, were the only types of employment open to women, keeping earning power low and women dependent upon men for life, particularly when children came into the picture.

A woman had virtually no identity apart from her husband. She could not sign a contract, sue, or own property. Let's consider for a moment how it would be if you were living in those times.

Imagine you have brought $50,000 into your marriage. Although you are still alive, your husband has designated in his will that the money—your money—shall go to his mistress, along with any property you owned prior to the marriage. Upon his death, you also learn that your children are no longer yours because their custody has also been given to the mistress. Imagine years of abuse, knowing if you were to seek a divorce, you would not be able to take your children with you. Back in the time of Abigail Adams, this was the law.

What was John Adams's response to Abigail's letter and request to "remember the ladies"? Well, despite the different times we live in today, it almost could have been written in current times.

I cannot but laugh. We know better than to repeal our Masculine systems. Altho they are in full Force, you know they are little more than Theory. We dare not exert our Power in its full Latitude. We are obliged to go fair, and softly, and in Practice you know We are the subjects. We have only the Name of Masters, and rather than give up this, which would compleatly subject Us to the Despotism of the Peticoat I hope General Washington, and all our brave Heroes would fight.[2]

Women represent 51 percent of the U.S. population and with all the gains made, still live without the benefits of constitutional equality. Although the United States was founded on the belief that freedom is a distinct human right, its Constitution was written by men and for men only. The vote, the Nineteenth Amendment, is the only guaranteed constitutional right women have.

The vast majority of Americans believe women are included in the U.S. Constitution guaranteeing equal rights. That is not correct. The fact is the majority of this country's citizenry does not have constitutional equality. Only men do.

Ruth Bader Ginsburg made it clear:

Every constitution written since the end of World War II includes a provision that men and women are citizens of equal stature. Ours does not. I have three granddaughters. I'd like them to be able to take out their Constitution and say here is a basic premise of our system, that men and women are persons of equal citizenship stature.[3]

Twenty-seven amendments to the U.S. Constitution are fully recognized at this time, two of which are about alcohol use, one on gun ownership, and one about Congressional pay. The Equal Rights

Amendment (ERA) will finally put women in the U. S. Constitution—protecting all Americans, regardless of gender, from discrimination on account of sex.

Now that the required thirty-eight states have ratified the ERA, the 117th Congress, both the Senate and the House, introduced joint resolutions in January of 2021, to eliminate the arbitrary deadline that was added to the amendment in the 1970s.

So, although we have an amendment that addresses pay for members of Congress, which by the way took more than 200 years to pass, women go to work every day and receive paychecks that, on average, are at least 20 percent less than white male counterparts. Women of color receive far less. By the end of a career, this pay difference amounts to hundreds of thousands of dollars and more, putting women and their families' financial security at risk and many women living in poverty.

We commonly hear of three waves of feminism; however, the fact is that women have never stopped working to create gender equality and eliminate institutionalized sexism that keeps unfair practices like unequal pay in place. Thank goodness for them all—the ones we will never know of and the ones we call "firsts." We stand on all their shoulders.

ATHLETES

All-American Girls Professional Baseball League—AAGPBL (1943-1954)

Between 1943 and 1954, more than 500 women played professional baseball in the AAGPBL. The league has been noted for kicking off women's professional sports in the United States with a million fans in attendance in 1948.[4]

Chicago Cubs owner Philip K. Wrigley and founder of the AAGPBL was not a feminist by any means, requiring the players to wear lipstick and short skirts. Off the field, players had to attend charm school and were not allowed to wear pants or drink alcohol.

Considered one of the best athletes of her time, Dorothy "Dottie" Kamenshek played in ten seasons for the AAGPBL and was named to the All-Star team seven of seven seasons an All-Star game was played. Sophie Kurys, Jean Faut, Dorothy "Snooky" Harrell, Mary "Bonnie" Baker, Ann Harnett, and Shirley Stovroff are a few of the women who loved and played baseball for the league, and according to Lavonne "Pepper" Paire, "would rather play ball than eat."

The popular movie *A League of Their Own* directed by Penny Marshall is a fictionalized account of the early years of the AAGPBL. In 2012, *A League of Their Own*, was added to the National Film Registry by the Library of Congress for preservation, citing it as a "culturally, historically, or aesthetically significant" film.[5]

Mo'ne Davis (2001–)

Davis was thirteen when she pitched a shutout in the 2014 Little League World Series. She was also the first Little League baseball player featured on the cover of *Sports Illustrated*.

I, and many of my peers, grew up in the 1950s and 1960s at a time when girls who played sports were called tomboys or worse. I still hear athletic girls called tomboys from time to time, although thankfully not nearly as much. We were, and they are, simply girls who, like some boys, love to play games, including ones with bats and balls.

Five decades after my sisters and I played sports in school, I was oftentimes teary-eyed watching my daughter play softball, basketball, and soccer when she was a child and field hockey throughout her middle and high school years. They were goose-bump moments for me. Female athletes at her school are highly thought of, and for that, I am thankful to all those who came before like Kamenshek, Stovroff, Davis, and my sisters, who played for the love of the game, like the boys.

ASTRONAUTS

Jerry Cobb (1931-2019)

Jerry Cobb was sixteen when she obtained her pilot's license. She was passionate about two things: space and becoming an astronaut.

In 1959, Cobb took a series of tests to qualify for the U.S. astronaut program. She passed them all, as did a dozen other women following in her footsteps. Unfortunately, for this era of female candidates, NASA ended the women's program, along with Jerry Cobb's path to space.

Russia would go on to become the first country to send a female astronaut, Valentina Tereshkova, into space in 1963. It would take another twenty years before the United States would follow suit and send Sally Ride into space.

Sally Ride (1951–2012)

A number of years ago, my daughter and I flew to Ohio to meet Sally Ride, astronaut and physicist, who in 1983 became the first female U.S. astronaut. I was so thrilled my daughter was able to meet Ride, the first American woman to break down another important barrier.

I thanked Ride for all she did to inspire so many girls and women to pursue science as a major in school and as a career. As she spoke that day to hundreds of young girls about science and space, her face beamed with pride and joy. She shared experiences that few people will ever experience, opportunities denied so many women before her. Today, more than fifty American women have flown in space.

Mae Jemison (1956–)

Mae Jemison is a chemical engineer, graduating from Stanford University, and a doctor, graduating from Cornell University. She is also the first African American woman to be launched into space on the space shuttle *Endeavour*, on September 12, 1992.

Ellen Ochoa (1958–)

Ellen Ochoa, also an engineer, became the first Hispanic woman to be launched into space. She holds both a master's and a doctoral degree from Stanford. Ochoa has been a part of four space flight crews, her first onboard the space shuttle *Discovery* in 1993.

One great accomplishment inspires and opens the door, and in some cases the world, for others.

"OUTSPOKEN" WOMEN

Ann Hibbins (died 1656)

In the mid-1600s in Boston, Ann Hibbins spoke publicly about a carpenter who had done work in her home she claimed was shoddy. At this time, only men were to speak out in public about family affairs. In 1656, Hibbins was executed as a witch, as were other women for expressing themselves in an "unconventional" way.

Still today, centuries later, women endure threats and harassment for stepping into male-dominated and unconventional fields.

Lynn Povich (1943–)

In March 1970, Lynn Povich and forty-five other degreed women at *Newsweek* filed a gender discrimination suit against the magazine, the first suit of its kind in the media. Only women were hired as researchers at *Newsweek* and rarely promoted. Regardless of education or experience, men were the writers and editors at *Newsweek*.

The *Newsweek* women met in secret for months, sometimes in the bathroom, fearful they would lose their jobs if discovered. Their complaint with the Equal Employment Opportunity Commission created an avalanche of suits at many major publications, because women were discriminated against throughout the industry, and paved the way for women to become writers. Povich would go on to become the first woman senior editor at *Newsweek*.

I went to the St. Louis Jewish Book Festival in 2013 to hear and hopefully meet Lynn Povich. Povich was a featured speaker talking about her new book at the time, *The Good Girls Revolt: How the Women of Newsweek Sued Their Bosses and Changed the Workplace*.

I loved her talk and made my way to her book signing table the last few minutes she was speaking so I might get a couple of minutes with her before the crowd showed up. It worked, and I got some time with Povich privately; however, I wanted to learn more. So I reached out to her in 2014 and asked if she would be willing to chat with me a bit more. I wanted to learn more about her and the lawsuit and get her perspective on a few key questions. I was thrilled when she said yes to my request and that I would be speaking with her again to learn more about this important time in history.

Povich shared with me how she was inspired to write about what made each woman at *Newsweek* wake up to their inequality. For some, it was being part of the women's revolution, challenging female roles in society: "I'm more than what I've been told I am." For others, it was fighting the injustice of the system: "Things don't have to be this way."

Other women, before the suit, had already left *Newsweek* to pursue writing careers after being denied the opportunity to write for the magazine, including Nora Ephron, Ellen Goodman, Jane Bryant Quinn, and Susan Brownmiller. Their departures were a good, hard lesson for *Newsweek* and demonstrate the tremendous loss for us all when we limit where people can go and what they do.

Today Povich is most interested in restructuring the workplace so that it is better for women and men. She optimistically shared, "I have great hopes in young men today because many of their best friends are women, and they want to be far more involved in raising their children than my father's generation."

Julie DiCaro (1973–)

Julie DiCaro, an anchor of a Chicago sports radio station, was called the C-word in 2006 on a sports blog. DiCaro had commented on the Cubs lineup and received this response, "Why would you bat Todd Walker second, you filthy cunt?"[6]

Nine years later things picked up steam during the time of an athlete's rape investigation. Here are some of the tweets DiCaro received:[7]

> Hopefully this skank Julie DeCarro[sic] is Bill Cosby's next victim. That would be classic.

> One of the Blackhawks players should beat you to death with their hockey stick like the WHORE you are cunt.

> F_ _ _ this dumb c_ _ _.

DiCaro had been raped. One of the tweets said, "I hope you get raped again."

Jen Lada (1981–)

In 2015, Jen Lada at ESPN spoke of an email she had received:

> A viewer emailed me saying the only reason I had my job was because I had used my big mouth to service my boss and male colleagues. When I responded that such vulgarity toward women set a terrible example for his young child (who was prominently featured in the man's Twitter and Facebook profiles) he replied that his son and his middle school-aged friends agreed and were laughing at me while watching as well.[8]

Sandra Fluke (1981–)

In 2012, Sandra Fluke was a thirty-year-old Georgetown University law student asked by Democrats to speak at a hearing by the House Oversight and Government Reform Committee regarding Conscience Clause exceptions in health care. Only men were on the committee and the hearing she was invited to would address contraception coverage. The Conscience Clause would make it possible for church organizations to refuse to cover contraception for their employees.

This was Rush Limbaugh's opinion on Ms. Fluke attending:

> What does it say about the college coed Susan Fluke, who goes before a congressional committee and essentially says that she must be paid to have sex, what does that make her? It makes her a slut, right? It makes her a prostitute. She wants to be paid to have sex. She's having so much sex she can't afford the contraception. She wants you and me and the taxpayers to pay her to have sex.[9]

No additional words are needed here other than to say that Limbaugh's radio show is one of the most popular radio shows ever.

Have we made progress since Anne Hibbins complained publicly and was subsequently burned at the stake? Yes—and it still comes with risk.

AUTHORS

Mary Wollstonecraft (1759–1797)

In 1792 Mary Wollstonecraft published *A Vindication of the Rights of Woman*, a book that would become important to the work of nineteenth-century women's rights activists. The book challenged the assumed inferiority of women, attributing any appearance of women's inferiority to the fact that women were denied an education. She was ridiculed by the president of Yale University, who claimed Wollstonecraft was a woman of poor character because she had chosen not to marry. Wollstonecraft's daughter, Mary Shelley, would go on to write *Frankenstein*.

Betty Friedan (1921–2006)

Almost two hundred years later, Betty Friedan wrote *The Feminine Mystique* (1963), which created what many refer to as the "second wave" of feminism. In her book, Friedan challenged the long-held belief that women were fulfilled only by assuming the roles of wife and mother. She gave a name to the guilt, anxiety, and depression so many women felt for wanting more than a husband, children, and home to care for. Women, who did not work outside of the home, finally had a name for the feelings many were experiencing. They weren't going crazy, and they were not alone.[10]

Friedan's book was timely in the sixties and an important piece of the puzzle for me as a young feminist and daughter who had lost her mother early. My mother was the valedictorian of her class, a star athlete, and outspoken as a child and as a mother. Did she want a career also, and if so, what would she have chosen to do?

Daphne Rose Kingma, author of *The Future of Love* and *The Men We Never Knew,* asked me one day after learning my mother died of stomach cancer, "What couldn't your mother stomach?" I'll never know the answer to that, of course, and what I do know is my mother loved her family more than anything in the world, like many of us with careers and families, women and men alike.

Generations past, including my own, moved women into the work-force in record numbers, and we are inching our way to the top, to equal pay, leadership roles, and opportunities. One of the biggest hurdles for women remains. Until we equalize the work at home, we will forever be chasing equality outside of it.

Back in the late nineties my younger sister Cathy worked and lived in New York City, in the upper west side. I dialed her number one day—or I thought I did—to chat.

I got a recording that clearly wasn't my sister, so I hung up. However, my heart started racing. Did I hear what I think I heard? "This is the home of Betty Frie_____." That's about when I hung up the first time, cutting off the last part of the name. Betty Frie _____ . Could it be? I had to find out.

I called back and this is what I heard: "This is the home of Betty Friedan. She is not here as she is in her Washington D.C. home and you can reach her at _____ ," and the number followed. Wow, Betty Friedan, author of *The Feminine Mystique*. Could this really be happening? I had inadvertently changed the order of my sister's number—and got Betty Friedan's. What are the odds?

Of course, I had to call the D.C. number. When I did, I got another recording. I left a message stating my name and a project I was working on at the time. I was looking at how major newspapers in St. Louis treated women versus men. If a woman was featured on the front page, she was typically in a small story below the fold or had just been murdered. There were few front-page stories featuring women leaders in the world, the country, or St. Louis. It was getting on my nerves to such an extent that I put hundreds of hours into the research and then presented my findings to each newspaper.

Within a couple of days of leaving a message at Friedan's D.C. number, my assistant came into my office and said Betty Friedan's office was on the phone. A bit nervously, I took the call and said hello. A woman told me that Betty Friedan would like to speak with me and asked my availability for a call. Then, at our scheduled time, I called and personally talked with Betty Friedan.

It was soon clear that she was having difficulty hearing me, so I switched gears away from my project and turned the call into one of appreciation for her work, her book, and the difference she made. It wasn't flawless, Friedan's life and work, as none of us are. Yet she shook up America and gave many women a sense of sanity for wanting something other than family life to care for. That is one telephone call I will always remember.

BUSINESS LEADER

Maxine Clark (1949–)

One of the many wonderful people I had the privilege of working with during my twenty-five-year corporate career, was Maxine Clark, at a division of May Company in the 1980s. Clark would go on to begin her own company, the extraordinarily successful Build-a-Bear Workshop, with stores throughout the world.

I chatted with Clark in 2015. I wanted to get her perspective on how we close that persistent numbers gap between female and male leaders in corporate America and government.

I enjoyed hearing about her career, from her early years in retail starting out on the East Coast. She told me she never felt discriminated against, although others have told her she was. She would get into a job, and her curiosity would take over. She studied every department to fully understand her role and paid special attention to how departments worked together. In this way, she knew the overall operation, what worked and what didn't, and how to make things better—which she did a lot over the years.

I came into a division of May Company as a staff analyst, and although I enjoyed the data analysis part of my job, it was a bit too hands-off the business to keep my interest for too much longer. So I was happy when, about a year into the job, Clark asked me to move into advertising. I will always be thankful to her for supporting me and many other women and men along her way. She always took the time to do that.

When we spoke in 2015, Clark said something that particularly resonated with me. She said often you will see a poorly performing company bring on a woman to clean things up and turn it around. Likewise, she said, "It is time for a woman to be president. We've tried about everything else. We have to look at the world through a different set of eyes. It's been done in other countries. Why can't we?"

PRESIDENTIAL CANDIDATES

Victoria Woodhull (1838–1927)

In 1872, Victoria Woodhull was the first woman to run for president of the United States. She fought for both women's rights and labor reform. She ran as an Equal Rights Party candidate in 1872—almost fifty years before women got the right to vote. You gotta love it!

Victoria Woodhull once said, "They cannot roll back the rising tide of reform. The world moves." Yes, it does although sometimes rather slowly. It would take another 145 years in the United States before a woman would become a nominee for president of a major U.S. party.

Shirley Chisholm (1924–2005)

Shirley Chisholm was the first black woman elected to the U.S. Congress, serving seven terms in New York. In 1972, Chisholm became the first African American woman to run for president of the United States, in one of the two major parties. She was prohibited from participating in the primary debates. After taking legal action she was allowed to make one speech.

She recognized, in her own words, the "double handicap" she had being both black and female. Her years in public life were largely dedicated to ending racial and gender inequality, poverty, and the Vietnam War.

Chisholm would go on to say about her legacy, "I want to be remembered as a woman . . . who dared to be a catalyst of change."[11] That she most certainly was.

Hillary Rodham Clinton (1947–)

After becoming the first female nominee of a major party, Clinton would go on to win the popular vote by about 3 million votes in the 2016 election. This is quite remarkable given she did so despite misogyny and sexism, the unprecedented FBI/James Comey announcement that the FBI would be reopening their investigation into the Clinton emails eleven days before the election, and Russian interference to support Donald Trump. We didn't quite see that final crack in the glass ceiling, but thanks to Clinton we got so much closer. We also changed Congress forever.

The 2018 mid-term election was extraordinary for the country as diverse representation grew significantly. The 116th U.S. Congress added twenty women and lots of firsts: the first Muslim women (Ilhan Omar and Rashida Tlaib), the first Native American women (Sharice Davids and Deb Haaland), the first Latina representatives from Texas (Veronica Escobar and Sylvia Garcia), the first transgender person elected in Virginia (Danica Roem), and the first female senator ever elected in Tennessee (Marsha Blackburn).

The 2020 election also brought more women running for the White House than ever before. One of those was Marianne Williamson, spiritual leader, and *New York Times* best-selling author.

I lobbied Congress with Williamson for a Department of Peace several years ago. There were many wonderful people there, including Deepak Chopra, Michael Beckwith, Nicole Brown Simpson's sister, Tanya Brown, and others.

Years after this memorable experience, I was Missouri co-chair for Room to Read, a global, nonprofit organization dedicated to the education of children in Africa and Asia, with a special program to ensure girls stay in school. In 2012, I learned Williamson was coming to St. Louis for an event. When I contacted the sponsor of that event and told her of the work I was doing with Room to Read, she was more than happy to contact Williamson to see if she would consider a special party following Williamson's event on behalf of Room to Read. She said yes.

I attended Williamson's event during the day, before our Room to Read party. She was quite inspiring. During the Q&A, I rose and asked her to consider running for president. Williamson spoke of love and healing, collaboration, and peaceful solutions. Later that day at our private Room to Read party, I sat with Williamson for a bit. We talked about loss early in life, love, and world peace. It was a beautiful conversation with a heart-driven peace warrior, the kind of conversation the world could use more of.

CIVIL RIGHTS LEADERS

Rosa Parks (1913–2005)

In 1955, Rosa Parks refused to give up her seat to a white person on a bus in Montgomery, Alabama. She was arrested. This launched the Montgomery bus boycott and a Supreme Court decision that declared the laws that segregated buses to be unconstitutional. She was called "the first lady of civil rights" and "the mother of the freedom movement" by the U.S. Congress.

Imagine the courage it took to tell a white bus driver in the 1950s, in the Deep South, you're not going to be giving up your seat for the white person who got on the bus after you. Parks received the Presidential Medal of Freedom and the Congressional Gold Medal. A statue of Parks resides in the U.S. Capitol's National Statuary Hall. She became the first woman, and third nongovernment official, upon her death, to lie in honor at the Capitol Rotunda.

She told us:

> People always say that I didn't give up my seat because I was tired, but that isn't true. I was not tired physically, or no more

tired than I usually was at the end of a working day. I was not old, although some people have an image of me as being old then. I was forty-two. No, the only tired I was, was tired of giving in.[12]

When I was fifteen, in the early 1970s, my first boyfriend was African American and from a small town in Missouri. Hanging out together was a secretive thing in the early seventies. I was called a variety of ugly racist things by some who did see us together. Even at that young age, I was growing tired of a world that judged so harshly and limited opportunities for people because of gender and race.

Missouri celebrates Rosa Parks Day on February 4, her birthday. That celebration helps me positively rewrite my experience of being called derogatory names in a small town in Missouri simply for caring for someone who had a different skin color than my own.

Fannie Lou Hamer (1917-1979)

The last of twenty children, Fannie Lou Hamer picked cotton at the age of six years old, alongside her parents and siblings on a farm in Mississippi.[13] Raised in poverty, she would go on to help thousands of African Americans register to vote and co-found organizations supporting women and people of color to vote and run for office.

She, along with other women, was arrested for sitting in a white-only restaurant in Charleston, South Carolina. While in jail, the women were severely beaten, causing Hamer lifelong eye, kidney, and leg issues.

Hamer would go on to say, "I'm sick and tired of being sick and tired." Sexism and racism, which Fannie Lou Hamer endured both of, are at the very least, exhausting.

WOMEN'S RIGHTS LEADERS

Sojourner Truth (1797–1883)

Sojourner Truth was an abolitionist and women's rights activist. You know that question, "If you could talk to a famous person from history, who would it be?" For me, that's Sojourner Truth.

The extraordinary contributions she would make after living years in slavery, enduring violence, hard labor, and separation from her children, remind us of the inhumane beginnings of the United States and the courageous paths some would choose risking their own lives to make things right for those to come.[14]

She delivered her famous "Ain't I a Woman" speech in 1851 at the Ohio Women's Rights Convention in Akron, Ohio. Truth's speech might have been the first public statement regarding the intersection of our multiple identities, that for some can create opportunities while for others insufferable challenges.

Truth would be included in the *Smithsonian* magazine's list of the "100 Most Significant Americans of All Time" in 2014.

One of my favorite quotes is by Sojourner Truth:

> *If women want any rights more than they's got, why don't they just take them, and not be talking about it.*

Now there's an idea.

Justice Ruth Bader Ginsburg (1933–2020)

Imagine attending both Harvard Law School and Columbia Law School, tying for first place in your class, and working on both the Harvard and Columbia Law Reviews. Then with recommendations, one from a future dean, and applying to a dozen law firms, you come up empty handed—not one job offer. Why? Not one firm, no matter the résumé, would hire a female attorney.

Two words come to mind when I think about all these firms that passed on the extraordinary RBG because of her gender—big mistake!

Thank goodness because we probably would never have seen the likes of the "notorious" Justice Ruth Bader Ginsburg we have come to know and love. Her passion for equality, incredible work ethic, and demeanor set her apart. She worked tirelessly for decades to level the playing field for women and men, for African Americans, LGBTQ+ and immigrants. Justice Ginsburg has become one of the great women's rights advocates and humanitarians of our time.

In her words:

We should not be held back from pursuing our full talents, from contributing what we could contribute to the society, because we fit into a certain mold . . . because we belong to a group that historically has been the object of discrimination.[15]

and . . .

You can disagree without being disagreeable.[16]

It is hard to imagine the Supreme Court and the country without Justice Ruth Bader Ginsburg. Given her recent death, we must now do so. Her last wish, told to her granddaughter, was that she not be replaced until a "new president is installed."

That request was not honored. Judge Amy Coney Barrett was nominated by President Donald Trump in September of 2020, just weeks before the 2020 election, despite the fact a Republican-led Senate refused to conduct a hearing for President Obama's nominee, Merrick Garland, eight months before the 2016 election. The reason Senator Mitch McConnell stated was, "The American people are about to weigh in on who is going to be the president. And that's the person, whoever that may be, who ought to be making this appointment."

Three days before the 2020 election, President Trump stated at a rally, "If we win on Tuesday or thank you very much Supreme Court, shortly thereafter." In other words, given his last Supreme Court appointee, he is suggesting that a decision by the Court, if needed, would go in his favor.

After a deep breath, I ask myself, what would RBG do? My answer—get back to work.

Gloria Feldt (1942–)

Gloria Feldt, former president of Planned Parenthood Federation of America, is a women's rights activist and the best-selling author of *No Excuses*. When she accepted the position at Planned Parenthood, Feldt never even thought of negotiating her salary. Today, along with her team at Take the Lead, she is dedicated to bringing gender parity, in both numbers and pay, to leadership roles in corporate America by 2025.

When I had the wonderful opportunity to meet with Feldt a few years ago, I shared with her how her book had inspired me and how it had shown me that I had stopped envisioning myself past the vice president position in my company. I remember clearly in my corporate days saying to myself, I want to be a vice president one day—not president, vice president.

I didn't like the lifestyle of top leaders of companies in those days: lots of after-hour schmoozing and weekday and weekend golf games. I preferred to work and then be with my family after hours. Of course, I understand today I could have changed the model and been president on my own terms.

"We all have our missteps and self-doubts," she told me that day, herself included. "To change power paradigms is very difficult. We have to give people something to see it differently. Until we have more women at the top, we'll fight the same battles again and again." This is why Feldt works with leaders today—to change the power paradigms.

She went on to say, "Not everyone will be on board, but 70 percent of women are, and that's all it will take for change. It is time to change the paradigm on how we are fighting the battles."

I have joined Feldt for her online events, Take the Lead Happy Hours, to learn and continue, as she said in her book *No Excuses*, "to move the fulcrum, finally, to abundant justice and full equality so that women can at least lead unlimited lives."

On one occasion Gloria Steinem joined the online Take the Lead event. She took several questions, one of which was mine regarding male violence. She agreed that the violence women endure at the hands of men (mostly men they know) is the most pressing problem we face.

Women must consider the safety factor in just about everything they do. Traveling, walking day or night, a cab or rideshare, going to college, jogging, parking in a garage, a date, a marriage—all can be lethal activities for women. And being at home is the most dangerous place of all for women. The majority of women killed worldwide in 2017, approximately 58 percent, were killed by family members or partners.[11]

Albert Einstein said, "Any intelligent fool can make things bigger and more complex. It takes a touch of genius—and a lot of courage—to move in the opposite direction."

Women's history is mostly untold, so I took some time to google firsts in their fields and women's rights activists who are Native American, Hispanic, Asian, Indian, African American, and on and on. I read dozens of stories.

History serves so many purposes. As I looked back to the women who have most inspired me, those on the preceding pages, as well as many others, I see a delicate thread connecting us—delicate because had they chosen a different path, the status quo, my life, my daughter's life, our lives might be quite different today.

Throughout history, females have been denied education (and still are), the right to own property (and still are), the right to vote (and still are), the right to make decisions about their own health care (and still are), and the right to work outside of the home (and still are). Despite the inequalities, limited opportunities, and access to resources, women have always made extraordinary contributions to their families, communities, nations, and the world. Now imagine a world where inequality no longer exists. Imagine the possibilities then. Ending poverty, disrupting climate change, peace perhaps?

In January 2017 in Washington, D.C., we made history when approximately half a million of us came together, women, men, and children, for the Women's March, the largest protest in U.S. history in a single day. It is estimated a total of 5 million people marched that day around the world to protest legislation that would harm women, immigrants, health care, the environment, LGBTQ+ rights, racial equality, workers' rights, and religious freedom.

I was so proud of my family who flew in for the march from several different states. I only wish my daughter had been able to join us. She was completing her master's degree abroad, a reality for her because so many girls and women before us stood for the right to be educated when the norms of their time said otherwise.

I felt them all with us that cold, yet beautiful day in D.C., as people from around the world walked peacefully, shoulder to shoulder, heart to heart. The march solidified for me, even more so, the purpose of this book. Equality and peace go hand in hand. When millions of people can come together, given such adversity and injustice in the world, and do so peacefully, everything is possible. All the institutions in the world, mostly designed by men, for men, can be redesigned by all for all.

E pluribus unum. Out of many, one.

Holding each person in the space of infinite possibilities, not to something ascribed to them at birth, we become the people who can solve our greatest challenges, from personal squabbles at home, at school, and work, through government, nation by nation.

Goodness and greatness come not from a specific gender or sexual orientation, race or religion, or nationality. Goodness and greatness come from the heart. We each have one of those. Allowing every human being their full freedom and equal access to opportunities and resources will bring about the peace and prosperity we want to see and experience in the world.

Our journey to equality is like a mosaic, with each of us a vital piece to its completion. We have much work to do, and maybe none of us alive today will see the day when gender equality is our reality.

However, there's nothing better than knowing you played your part, took a stand, and followed through. All those to come will be the benefactors of your choices. And who knows? You might even be one of the firsts in a list of firsts to come.

History also provides us with important lessons. One of the most important is the actions that have come from love, compassion, and kindness, provide the best path forward.

We've seen the destruction and divisiveness that come from hate, prejudice, exclusion, lies, corruption, and greed. And we've seen how greatness, defined by goodness, is what supports the individual, the family, an organization, a community, a nation, and the world to flourish.

As the Persian poet Rumi said centuries ago, "Your heart knows the way. Run in that direction."

The heart never lies, never cheats, never hates, never kills, never excludes, and never blames. Back to the heart, I like to say. That's where our best decisions can be made; the ones that are best for all concerned.

FOUR

The Facts Aren't Pretty: Nevertheless We Persist!

The truth will set you free.
But first it will piss you off.

—Gloria Steinem

The sentiment of this quote by Gloria Steinem becomes the truth for many women. With age can come a freedom we never knew as girls, when our lives were limited; our physical appearance was deemed more important than our abilities or brainpower; and parents, teachers, and bosses showed a clear preference for the males around us. It's hard not to be angry about your own experiences and the ongoing plight of our sisters, daughters, nieces, mothers, and grandmothers around the world.

The life of a female, still today, can be quite different from the life of her brother, although they share the same parents, home, and time

47

in history. It's almost as though there is one of those directional signs that says females go this way, males go that way. And the world responds to us according to our ascribed gender well before it ever gets to know anything about us.

Let's take a closer look at some ways this plays out in the world:

EDUCATION

Girls are more likely to never attend a day of school.

- 130 million six- to seventeen-year-old girls are not in school—girls are four times more likely to be out of school than boys.[1]

- Two-thirds of the 781 million illiterate adults—496 million—are female.[2]

Females who attend school reinvest 90% of their income into their families versus 30-40% of income invested in families by males.[3] Increasing the number of girls in school by 10% increases a country's gross domestic product by 3%. That's a big return on ensuring all children get an education.

POVERTY

Women are more likely to live in poverty.

- Women are paid less than white men for the same work with less job security.[4]

- Women have longer workdays and do two times more unpaid work than men.[5]

▸ 2.5 million U.S. children will be brought out of poverty when
    women are paid equal to men.[6]

Equal pay for women in the United States would cut the poverty
rate in half for employed women and their children and add more than
$500 billion of income to the U.S. economy.[7]

VIOLENCE

**Seven of ten females worldwide experience physical and/or
sexual abuse by an intimate partner.[8]**

▸ Domestic violence in the United States is the leading cause of
    injury to women—more than car accidents, muggings, and
    rape combined.[9]

▸ Three women are murdered every day in the United States.[10]

▸ Every nine seconds a woman is beaten.[11]

▸ Every six minutes a woman is raped in the United States; 1 in 5
    American women will be raped in her lifetime.[12]

▸ More than 40% of African American women experience domestic
    violence (versus 31% of all women) and are 2.5 times more likely
    to be killed by men than white women.[13]

▸ Transgender people of color are 2.6 times more likely to be a
    victim of intimate partner violence.[14]

▸ Women with disabilities are 40% more likely to be a victim of intimate partner violence than women without a disability.[15]

▸ The leading cause of death for pregnant women in the United States is intimate partners.[16]

▸ More than one in five female undergraduate students are sexually assaulted at American universities.[17]

▸ One-third of female U.S. soldiers are raped by U.S. military men.[18]

▸ 13% of rape survivors will attempt suicide, 94% experience post-traumatic stress disorder, whereas 99% of those who commit sexual assault will go free.[19]

"Women worldwide, ages fifteen through forty-four, are more likely to die or be maimed because of male violence than because of cancer, malaria, war, and traffic accidents combined."[20]

FEMALE GENITAL CUTTING

▸ 200 million females have undergone female genital cutting, with 3 million at risk each year.[21]

CHILDHOOD MARRIAGE

▸ Every day 37,000 girls under eighteen are married.[22]

▸ 400 million women, between the ages of twenty to forty-nine, were married before their eighteenth birthday.[23]

Most of the data available regarding childhood marriages look only at female minors. Male childhood marriages are consistently a fraction of female childhood marriages.

SEX SLAVERY

It is estimated that there are 40 million people in slavery today worldwide.[24]

- ▸ 71% of those enslaved are female.[25]

- ▸ 75% of human trafficking victims are female.[26]

ECONOMIC AND POLITICAL POWER

Women earn less than men in almost every occupation.

- ▸ For every dollar a white man earns, a woman earns about 80 cents.[27]

  - • Women of color are paid 63 cents.

  - • Native American women are paid 57 cents.

  - • Latina women are paid 54 cents.

  - • Asian women are paid 87 cents.

- ▸ A woman will earn $590,000 less than a man working from sixteen years of age to seventy.[28]

Women are significantly underrepresented in business and politics.

- 6% (33) of Fortune 500 companies have a female CEO; few of these are women of color.[29]

- About 24% of seats in the 2019 U.S. Congress are held by women: twenty-five of the one hundred in the Senate, 102 of the 435 in the House of Representatives.[30]

- 6–7% of all heads of state and prime ministers worldwide were women in 2018.[31]

In a Time of Pandemic

When you're already in a hole, a natural disaster or pandemic can only make it deeper and, in the case of COVID-19, much deeper. Women are facing human rights violations, some of which are endangering them more than the virus itself.

Domestic violence and severity are increasing worldwide due to the pandemic. With stay-at-home orders and growing financial stress, as was experienced with Ebola, women are enduring increased levels of violence in their homes with fewer services available to support them.

Most of the jobs that have been lost in the United States are in the service sector. These are jobs held mostly by women and are oftentimes lower-wage jobs that offer no health insurance or paid sick leave, leaving women particularly vulnerable. Hispanic women and women of color are affected the most.

Most single households with children in the United States are headed by women. Without daycare options and with schools closed, going back to work is not an option. This has added significant financial hardship to families, also risking future opportunities and career growth for women. As a result, we may see a tremendous setback in female leadership in business for decades to come.

Routine health-care services such as maternity and reproductive health, along with childhood vaccinations, are now even more limited for women worldwide. When family planning services are not accessible, unplanned pregnancies and poverty are around the corner.

In the 1830s Sarah Moore Grimke kicked off this wild notion that women's rights are not any different than the rights of men by saying, "I know nothing of man's rights, or woman's rights; human rights are all that I recognize."

About 150 years later, Hillary Clinton said it again. Speaking before the United Nations Fourth World Conference on Women in Beijing, she said these important words, "If there is one message that echoes forth from this conference, let it be that human rights are women's rights and women's rights are human rights, once and for all."[32]

Clinton followed with, "As long as discrimination and inequities remain so commonplace everywhere in the world, as long as girls and women are valued less, fed less, fed last, overworked, underpaid, not schooled, subjected to violence in and outside their homes—the potential of the human family to create a peaceful, prosperous world will not be realized."

So how much longer until we reach gender equality?

According to the World Economic Forum (WEF), it will take approximately a hundred years before we're there.[33] That's right, it will be another century before we close the global gender gap. In 2006, the WEF introduced the Global Gender Gap Index to track gender-based disparities between women and men over time. The report looks at four critical areas of our lives: education, politics, economy, and health.

The 2018 Global Gender Gap Report has some good and some not-so-good news. The fact the report exists is great news. The world is beginning to understand and pay attention to the extraordinary gains made in communities and countries as we move closer to gender equality. We know from the data that oppression of women is tied to higher rates of poverty, violence, and lack of economic growth.[34]

The 2018 Global Gender Gap Report tells us that collectively we are 68% of the way to gender equality, meaning there is a gender gap of 32 percent worldwide. So, we're about two-thirds of the way home. Although 89 of the 144 countries included in the report show some improvement, we are moving slowly toward gender equality.

The largest gender gap exists in Political Empowerment, with a world gap of 77.1%. This means we are only 23% of the way to political gender equality.

The Economic Participation and Opportunity gap is at 41.9%, which means we are only 58 percent of the way to economic gender equality.

The Educational Attainment and Health and Survival gaps are significantly less: 4.4 percent and 4.6 percent, respectively, which means we are about 95 percent of the way to gender equality on both of these key measures.

Where the two biggest gender gaps lie, political empowerment and economic opportunity, the WEF estimates another 107 years and 202 years, respectively, to close the gaps.

The top ten most gender-equal countries in the world as of 2018 include the following:

Country	Percent of Gender Gap Closed
1. Iceland	85.8%
2. Norway	83.5%
3. Sweden	82.2%
4. Finland	82.1%
5. Nicaragua	80.9%
6. Rwanda	80.4%
7. New Zealand	80.1%

8. Philippines   79.9%

9. Ireland   79.6%

10. Namibia   78.9%

The United States ranks number fifty-one, with a 72 percent gender gap closure score.

By regions of the world, here is a quick overview:

	Percent of Gender Gap Closed	Estimated Years to Close Gender Gap
Western Europe	75.8 %	61 years
North America	72.5 %	165 years
Latin America	70.8 %	74 years
Eastern Europe and Central Asia	70.7 %	124 years
East Asia and the Pacific	68.3 %	171 years
Sub-Saharan Africa	66.3 %	135 years
South Asia	65.8 %	70 years
Middle East and North Africa	60.2 %	153 years

Parliaments that include women take on different issues than mostly male-run parliaments. There is more legislation on health, education, child support, and discrimination, and when women are at the peace table, peace is more likely to last.[35]

Giving women farmers the same tools as men would increase crop yields and reduce hunger for up to 150 million people. "Women reinvest 90 percent of their earnings into their households—that's money spent on nutrition, food, health care, school, and income-generating activities—helping to break the cycle of intergenerational poverty."[36]

World leaders are learning that when girls and women are educated, safe, free to make their own decisions, and included in society, both economically and politically, the national economy improves. As the gender gap closes, child mortality rates go down, and poverty decreases significantly, as do illness and disease, violence, and the propensity for war. These are big reasons to make gender equality a top priority in every country.

I hope it's getting more clear that we cannot make progress with the most pressing challenges we face today when half of the world's population is at risk and held back. One factor that prevents greater progress is the lack of men speaking up about the epidemic rates of violence and the extraordinary double standards men benefit from at the expense of women. Men challenging other men is greatly needed.

Two courageous men speaking out today are Jackson Katz and Zaron Burnett III. Both are calling upon men to listen, learn, and be in action to help us end male violence.

Jackson Katz, author, filmmaker, and educator, asks an important question: "What's going on with men?" His Tedx talk *Violence Against Women—It's a Men's Issue* addresses what is at the source of epidemic rates of gender violence.[37] His Bystander Approach, used by the U.S. military and sports organizations, calls upon us to not sit idle when we hear sexist language, just as it is important that bystanders not sit idle when they hear racist or anti-Semitic language.

Men, when you hear a friend, family member, or colleague say something degrading about women, Katz offers these responses: "Hey, that's not funny," or "I don't appreciate that kind of talk," or "You're talking about my sister," or "Can we talk about something else" instead of laughing it off or pretending you didn't hear it.

Each of us can make a profound difference in reducing and eliminating sexist and hurtful language about women that fuels violence. Although it's not always easy to go up against male culture, Katz reminds us that with our silence, "We give our consent and become complicit."

Zaron Burnett III, investigative reporter and social commentator, writes about culture, politics, and race. Two great articles Burnett wrote are "A Gentleman's Guide to Rape Culture"[38] and "A Gentleman's Guide to the #MeToo Era."[39] Burnett does an excellent job of bringing men into the conversation to create greater awareness and understanding of male entitlement that affects women and their safety.

I had the extraordinary pleasure of speaking with Burnett one Sunday afternoon. He was born in Atlanta, Georgia, and now lives in Los Angeles. I was quite moved to learn about his passion for writing in the context of social change. "I am the son of a writer," he told me, "and so I grew up understanding the importance of writing, how it shapes and changes lives, and how it can take incremental changes and turn them into much bigger change over time."

We began our conversation talking about the Netflix series *When They See Us*, the story of five African American kids in 1989 who were wrongfully convicted of raping and beating a woman, almost to death, in Central Park. They spent years in jail fighting their convictions and were eventually exonerated in 2002, following the confession of a convicted murderer and serial rapist serving a life sentence. Ava DuVernay co-wrote and directed the series.

Burnett's insights and keen observations about the series are important in our understanding of social injustice. Here is what he had to say:

That series in particular is an accurate story that I've been aware of since it first occurred. Ava was able to show the machinations that are required for something like that to happen.

Instead of pointing a finger at something anomalous like the system, she showed the various slices that make it up and how they interlock to create the narratives of oppression. It wasn't that the system did it; people did it. People did this to other people. We get lost in wanting to point fingers and assign blame. The blame was in so many places. We need to look beyond blame and look at the actual process to understand it. You're left with this feeling of injustice and also with an understanding of how injustice occurs.

He went on to say, "Everyone's personal agenda intersects with the biases and incentives of culture. People are able to take advantage of dynamics of power or manipulation or coercion because of the system. But it's still individual actors. So it's that intersection that matters most."

Seeing so many parallels in how women are treated, I asked Burnett what he thought of the Supreme Court confirmation hearings for Brett Kavanaugh, following Dr. Christine Blasey Ford's allegation of sexual assault.

Burnett spoke of how enraging and horrifying, in equal measure, the hearings were.

It was so offensive the way the men in Congress were talking about it. I didn't expect so many Republican senators to put aside their personal feelings the way they did. They decided to put the agenda of party first and not even in a way that was good for the party. It was horrifying to see for what little gain they were willing to sacrifice their souls. Victims of sexual assault were unearthing the greatest trauma in their lives and they got the message that not only did it not matter; it was being dismissed.

He also pointed out:

Conservatives viewed it as a political game. They weren't able to see it as a human moment. We have gamified politics to the point that humanity gets turned into chips and characters. Victims of assault were reliving trauma and having nightmares for someone's political gaming, for a seat on the Court. There was this terrible imbalance of what was being discussed versus real personal pain. You're angry at them, and your heart aches for them at the same time because they have lost their connection to humanity. I was bothered by how much pain there was and how much numbness there was. Both the pain and the numbness were horrifying.

Although these are tough topics, I also heard so much hope in Burnett's words as we spoke that day. He remains true to his mission to be that catalyst for change putting words out in the universe that spark perhaps anger first then create greater self-awareness and change.

Burnett gets some pretty ugly tweets in the wake of articles like "A Gentleman's Guide to Rape Culture" and "A Gentleman's Guide to the #MeToo Era." Even so, he enthusiastically told me he gets plenty of positive responses as well, and that is what gives him hope.

More men write to me and tell me it is really helpful. They say things like, 'I didn't see this when I first read it; you really opened my eyes.' Some shared that they had talked with different people in their lives—their mothers, sisters, girlfriends—about the articles and that they opened their eyes to things they just hadn't seen before.

Burnett views this as a strong indicator things are changing, especially among younger men.

> GenX men tend to be a little more reluctant, not that it is too late for them to change. They feel they know how things work and why they occur. Younger men are more flexible and are wanting to be their best selves, so they are more willing to take it on. GenX men are oftentimes convinced they know what their best selves look like until they meet a personal crisis or tragedy. Millennial men and GenZ men are very open and have had their opinions changed.

Earlier comments Burnett made in our conversation wrap it up beautifully.

> You can't disrupt the whole system, but you can get people to stop intersecting with it the way they have been, and that is where change occurs. We've seen it in other social dynamics like the *cancel* culture. What is considered acceptable can change very quickly if we can get enough people to say this is unacceptable and those people on the fence to say we're not doing this anymore. All we need to do is get enough people, and then those critical masses start to form naturally. There is hope in the process. If enough people say rape culture is real, then you can make traction.

In the article "A Gentleman's Guide To Rape Culture," Burnett provides what I see as the bottom line, "Rape culture is not about men versus women; it's also not about men having to protect women. The fight against rape culture is about ensuring equal dignity and respect for all. It's just that simple."

I agree wholeheartedly. That's where we need to head—more conversations about equal dignity and respect for all. It truly is that simple.

Jennifer Siebel Newsom is another courageous individual on a mission for girls and boys, women and men, to live unlimited, fair, and equal lives. Siebel Newsom graduated with honors from Stanford University and Stanford Graduate School of Business. She founded The Representation Project, an organization dedicated to eradicating social injustice caused by gendered stereotypes and norms.[40]

She produced two important films, *Miss Representation* and *The Mask You Live In*. *Miss Representation* sheds light on the media's role in reducing female value to their appearance and sexuality, devaluing their abilities and leadership potential. *The Mask You Live In* tells the story of boys who are forced to navigate their way through life with an unhealthy definition of what it means to be a man, disconnected from their feelings, dominating women, acting aggressively, and violently. These are two important films that increase awareness of how gender-based stereotypes, like racial stereotypes, do damage to the individual, the family, and society at large.

The world looks the way it does because each of us lives in it, women and men. As Gloria Steinem reminds us, "The future depends entirely on what each of us does every day."[41] It's not just what women do and it's not just what men do. It's what all of us do.

When I think of the possibilities for the individual and the world, as we move closer to full equality, my heart soars. I hope yours does as well.

For girls and women, that means freedom to choose their own destiny, to be educated, earn money, be safe, and become the leaders who are so desperately needed in the world. Nations become more peaceful and prosperous when women are included and have equal access to resources and opportunities.

For boys and men, that means their humanity is front and center. They are free to feel, process, and express their emotions. They are strong and able to handle life's adversities in peaceful and collaborative ways, bringing greater peace, well-being, and harmony to the planet.

And my heart is relieved as I think of all the violent news of the day that will be a thing of our past, the massive amounts of money that will be available to improve infrastructures, schools, and communities versus senseless wars, domestic, and community violence.

Let our hearts lead the way as we work together to create the end of inequality. There will be setbacks—no doubt about it.

Nevertheless, and as we always have, we will persist.

FIVE

Oh, the Stories We Tell

*It is only questioning what people take for granted,
what people hold to be true, that we can break through
the hypnosis of social conditioning.*

—Deepak Chopra

While waiting for an early dinner at a favorite restaurant one night, I was fortunate to sit next to an interesting man from New York, probably late thirties, early forties. Like myself and so many other people who live in the South, we are transplants, oftentimes from a colder climate, escaping ice and snow for sun and sand. He, too, had relocated to live in a warmer climate and less hectic environment.

During our two-hour conversation, he shared with me an important time in his life. He had a wonderful childhood and a loving family. During his high school years, his parents would always want to know about his girlfriends. Then in his twenties, he came out. When he told his parents he was gay, he was not surprised to find it was not welcome news. They have never asked about his relationships since.

He shared something with me that took me by surprise as to what the best part of coming out was for him. I assumed he would say something about feeling free to live a more authentic life, loving who he wanted to love, or something like that. What I heard was not even close.

Although it was a difficult time for him with his parents, he said the best part of coming out was that he didn't have to listen to men disparaging women to feel better about themselves. Apparently, to hang out with his heterosexual guy friends, that was part of the deal.

At some point in a conversation with his straight male friends, a remark denigrating women would be made. No one would challenge it, and they would laugh and continue on with the conversation. It was part of being "one of the guys," he told me. Yet, because he loved and respected his mother and sister, he knew it wasn't right. Now, living his authentic life, he had left that world behind—along with the guys who thought it was cool to disparage women—and was a happier and better person for it.

Jan Morris, a trans female, tells us in her book *Conundrum* the extent to which external forces shape behaviors, perceptions, and beliefs. Morris transitioned to female in her adult life after a career in the military and as a reporter. Then, in 2006, she wrote the book *Conundrum*, one of the first books about transsexuality.

Before her transition, Morris was a distinguished soldier in the British military and went on to become a reporter, climbing mountains and crossing deserts establishing herself as a historian of the British empire. She was happily married with several children, yet since childhood felt she was female in a male body. Here's what she said after transitioning:

> The more I was treated as a woman, the more woman I became. I adapted willy-nilly. If I was assumed to be incompetent at revers-ing cars, or opening bottles, oddly incompetent I found myself

becoming. If a case was thought too heavy for me, inexplicably I found it so myself.[1]

When I first read this, it reminded me a bit of the "transition" I went through as a young girl when my mother died. It was a palpable change in my home, one I can still feel to this day when I recall that time in my life. Abruptly the scale tipped from a wonderfully balanced, loving, and supportive environment to one more focused on competition, accomplishment, and getting a job done. On top of that, fewer words and fewer feelings were expressed.

Just as the man from New York took on a persona that wasn't real for him to be "one of the guys" and Morris became more "female" as was expected of her, I took on different attributes to fit in at home following my mother's death and at the office, where I found myself in mostly male circles as I moved up in rank. I shifted course and became what my new environment expected of me—less talk, less emotion, and lots of hard work, with my attention on the next accomplishment and promotion.

We grow up in a world that values a female and male experience differently and defines each rigidly. We look at human traits and label them as masculine and feminine and then ascribe them to our children based on an assigned gender at birth.

I think few would disagree that the traditionally defined feminine and masculine traits, such as empathy, caring, attentiveness, nurturing, and sensitivity (feminine) and ambition, goal-oriented, courage, independence, and self-assured (masculine) are equally important for all of us. In reality, however, boys are taught to err on the side of masculinity and girls to err on the side of femininity. We thereby create a self-fulfilling perpetuation of gender-based stereotypes and justification for many ill-conceived theories and so-called truths that define us and cultures around the world.

Human beings need access to all human emotions so that we can bring wholeness to our lives, our families, our communities, and our work. It's the only way to create a truly fulfilling and balanced life. We must have a balance from within before we can ever create it in the family, the organization, and the world, caring for self, one another, and the planet.

Way too often boys are raised and socialized to believe expressing feelings such as kindness, care, compassion, and sadness is a weakness when the opposite is true. Doing so makes us stronger. You can't be strong emotionally, empathic, and able to cope with life's challenges in a positive and meaningful way if you don't exercise that muscle. Physical strength is good for lifting. Emotional strength is vital for life—relationships, parenting, health, and career.

Similarly, way too often girls are taught to put the needs of others before their own, learning that self-sacrifice is their role in life. Anything else is selfish. The opposite is true. We can't care for our families and exclude ourselves from the family's well-being, or be a team player at work, and not express our own ideas and feelings. Unfortunately, there is a heavy price to pay when these rigid, binary, gender-defined lines are crossed.

Despite a parent's good intentions to raise their children equally, regardless of gender, it's not an easy thing to do. Millions of messages are received every day, sending girls and boys on different trajectories to live different lives. The "girl" and "boy" toys children are given teach different skill sets, as do assigned chores at home, after-school activities, TV programming, teachers, books, movies, peer pressure, and on and on it goes. And although we are making headway, with growing awareness of the disservice we do to our children when we raise them with gender-based stereotypes, we have much work to do.

Fortunately, we are seeing changes in the toy industry to stop making girl and boy toys. Why is this so important? At the earliest of ages, parents are unwittingly introducing serious disadvantages to their children's development by choosing toys based on a binary definition of who that child is.

Researcher Jeffrey Trawick-Smith, professor of early childhood education at the Center at Eastern Connecticut State University, conducts an annual toy study called Toys that Inspire Mindful Play and Nurture Imagination (TIMPANI).[2] He looks at the impact types of toys have on three important areas of development: thinking, learning, and problem-solving; social interaction; and creativity.

According to Professor Trawick-Smith, there are toys that have a positive impact on "children's thinking, interaction with peers, and creative expression," and there are toys that do not. He advises us to select toys based on how it impacts a child's play behavior across "social, intellectual, and creative areas of development." The highest-performing toy from the 2018 Timpani study was Magz Clix by Magz, a building, and stacking set with magnets that allow for sideways connections.

According to Trawick-Smith, the highest performing toys were those that elicited "problem-solving, social interaction, and creative expression," in both girls and boys. Toys that are oftentimes considered best for boys, such as vehicles and construction toys, actually elicited the highest-quality play among girls. The best approach to selecting toys for your children is to set aside any gender-based notions you might have and select toys that equally benefit girls and boys.

What children learn in school also has serious implications in their development and sense of self-esteem. As women are largely omitted from history books, children grow up learning little about the extraordinary contributions women have always made to society.

Myra and David Sadker wrote the book *Failing at Fairness* in 1995. It was revised in 2009 with Karen Zittleman and was called *Still Failing at Fairness*.[3]

In 1992, the Sadkers asked fourth, fifth, and sixth graders to name as many famous women and men as they could, in history or present day, excluding those in sports and entertainment, in five minutes. On average, the students provided the names of eleven men and three women. The lists of women included names like Mrs. Fields, Aunt Jemima, Mrs. Bush, Sarah Lee, and Judy Blume, whereas the male names were from history books.

Fifteen years later, in 2007, they repeated the study and asked elementary and secondary school students to list as many famous women and men as they could, excluding those in sports and entertainment. This time they instructed the students to also exclude the wives of U.S. presidents. On average, twelve men's names and five women's names were listed. The highest number of men listed was thirty-four, and for women, the highest number was nine, which was the same as it was in 1992.

The Sadkers tell us students "know little about women because their books tell them little." In one of the history books the Sadkers reviewed, 819 pages total, the references of women added up to less than one page.

This cheats our children of a quality and accurate education and instills early on an unhealthy, biased viewpoint that history-making is a male domain. We think that's the way it is. After all, isn't history the truth and all the facts? Clearly not.

Gerda Lerner was a brilliant historian who also wrote the screenplay for the movie *Black Like Me* (1961), the true story of a white journalist, John Howard Griffin, seeking to answer a question, "What is it like to experience discrimination based on skin color, something over which one has no control?" Earlier in his life, Griffin was a student in France when World War II began. He joined the French resistance and helped Jewish children escape to Britain, so he was no stranger to the brutality of prejudice and racism.

To find an answer to his question, Griffin took medication, used a sun lamp, and rubbed a stain into his skin to darken it. He then traveled into the Deep South of the United States for several weeks, during the time of racial segregation, to experience discrimination firsthand.

In Gerda Lerner's book *The Creation of Patriarchy*, she opens with a hypotheses. "It is the relationship of women to history which explains the nature of female subordination, the causes for women's cooperation in the process of their subordination, the conditions for their opposition to it, the rise of feminist consciousness."[4]

Lerner points out the difference between the unrecorded past, all the events of the past, and that which has been recorded, mostly by men. Because recorded history has left out half the population, marginalizing the work and contributions of women, it not only leaves out important people and events but also wildly distorts recorded history by way of their omission.

She observed profound changes in the consciousness of her Women's History students. Learning history that includes women changed their lives. Even if the experience was in a two-week seminar, Lerner saw a profound psychological effect on women participants.

I experienced this myself in my Women's Studies courses and in reading *The Red Tent* by Anita Diamante many years ago. The *Los Angeles Times* said in their review of *The Red Tent*, "By giving a voice to Dinah, one of the silent female characters in Genesis, the novel has struck a chord with women who may have felt left out of biblical history."[5] May have felt left out? There is no "may have" about it.

As I read *The Red Tent*, I remember feeling a physical sensation run through me, as though a new dimension had been added to my body. It was truly exhilarating. I had tears in my eyes because I finally felt a part of myself recognized and celebrated for the first time as I read the beautiful story of Dinah, daughter of Jacob and Leah. I suspect this is what Lerner was referring to when she spoke of a profound psychological effect the women in her Women's Studies program experienced.

The Book of Genesis tells the story of Jacob and his twelve sons. Dinah is barely mentioned and reduced to being raped, which may not even have happened. Diamante's book gives us a deep dive into Dinah's life and what might have happened, thereby providing a unique look into the lives of women of her time.

We see the same thing in film. The wonderful movie *Lion* is a good example. It is the true story of a young Indian boy who is separated from his brother at a busy train station and then taken to live in Australia, where he is adopted by an Australian couple. While in college he becomes determined to find his way back to his mother and brother in India, almost an impossible mission, given what little he could remember about his rural childhood home in an enormous country.

It's an amazing story and I loved the movie, yet I wondered what it would have been like had it been told through the mother's eyes or included more of her story. What was it like for her losing both her young sons the day the two of them went off together to the train station, neither returning. What did she do to find her sons? A different story it would have been and every bit as important.

We're so used to excluding the stories of women and their experiences and don't even question it. Such has been the case with almost all of history, with women included peripherally at best.

After reading *Mary Called Magdalene* by Margaret George, I had a discussion with a man, sharing how exciting it was to read about Mary from a woman's perspective. I saw an alternative perspective of Mary, not of a prostitute but of a disciple. Women, after all, have been falsely labeled sluts forever, when it would protect a man's position in some way or another. This book and its portrayal of a woman in history represented another one of those *Red Tent* moments for me.

The man I was sharing the book with knew I was a women's rights advocate and didn't appreciate an alternative viewpoint of Mary. His comment was, "Well, that fits your narrative, now doesn't it?" I was taken aback, shocked by his response. As he turned and walked away, I thought, "Well, all of recorded history fits your narrative. How special that must be."

I want all of us to have a *Red Tent* moment when we see ourselves in history and in the change-makers. I invite men to imagine, year after year, from elementary school on up, reading almost nothing about the contributions men have made to history. How different do you think you would be? How significant would you hold yourself, could you hold yourself? How different might society be, and would you still hold history to be the whole story and the truth?

My daughter has assured me there has been an improvement in history books today, yet I see the absence of women still in so many places. Street signs and holidays are named almost exclusively after men. We still have no women on U.S. currency, and although we thought Harriet Tubman was to be our first, the Trump administration delayed it until 2026.

This absence of women's history leads to a lack of women celebrated, honored, and respected in all domains. It continues to plague us, does a terrible disservice to female confidence, and teaches our children that men are the ones who make history, are to be believed more, considered more often, hired, and elected.

Might it explain our forty-six to zero record: forty-six male U.S. presidents and zero women. Not one single female elected president in the United States with women representing half the U.S. population, brainpower, and potential. We're so unused to seeing women making their way into recorded history that it distorts how we view women in the present. Many, still today, will vote for the most incompetent man because that feels more secure to them than a brilliant, highly experienced woman. After all, that's what history has led them to believe. I have a feeling Gerda Lerner would have some interesting and important insights on that as well.

Remember the good old hunter-gatherer societies we all learned about in school? In fact, these societies were quite egalitarian, where each role was equally valued, and oftentimes women went out on the hunt as well. As we evolved into agrarian societies, where wealth and resources were accumulated, egalitarianism morphed into a "farmer and his wife" construct. Both are working on the farm, yet she is reduced to her marital status, "the farmer's wife."

It's much like the nonfarming household, where one leaves the house to work (oftentimes a man) and the other stays in the house (oftentimes a woman) to work—caring for children and home. Yet he's "the provider," and she "doesn't work." The person taking care of the home and children provides every bit as much to the family, but yet again, her contributions are diminished by a perspective and language, shaped largely by a lifetime of seeing history in this same distorted way.

By contrast, when feminist anthropologists look at history or do their own data collection, Lerner tells us, they see a different picture. They see cultures where the different roles and tasks of women and men had no hint of domination or subordination. In fact, the tasks were seen as vital to survival, neither one more important than the other. And when it comes to those hunter-gatherer societies, it was the gatherers who provided most of the food for the family.

Even in more recent times, with more female journalists and historians than ever, Lerner points out that most of their mentors have been men. So along with their predecessors, they, too, write mostly about men. When they write about women, they write about women who do what men do and do it the way men do it.

In time, this, too, shall pass, as growing numbers of women are leaders in their industries. As a result, for example, we are seeing more movies centered on female leads, women not playing that supportive role, and roles that don't always include a romantic relationship. Hooray for Hollywood!

There is a tool you can use to see if a movie is female positive. It's called the Bechdel Test.[6] It defines a female-positive movie as having at least two named female characters who converse about something other than a man. I loved learning about the Bechdel Test from my daughter who checks it when she looks for a movie to see. That's progress!

Let's take a look at another set of stories we have all been told.

Cordelia Fine is a professor and author of *Delusions of Gender, How Our Minds, Society and Neurosexism Create Difference*.[7] In 2018 she was awarded the Edinburgh Medal, which is given to "women and men of science who have made a significant contribution to the understanding and well-being of humanity."

In *Delusions of Gender*, Fine disputes the long-held belief of differences in female and male brains, which many have claimed make women best suited for some roles and men best suited for others. In Fine's fascinating book she shares quotes by well-established men in their fields during different eras—like this one from Thomas Gisborne, who writes in his best-selling book, *An Enquiry into the Duties of the Female Sex* (1797):

> The science of legislation, of jurisprudence, of political economy; the conduct of government in all its executive functions; these and other studies, pursuits, and occupations, assigned chiefly or entirely to men, demand the efforts of a mind endued with the powers of close and comprehensive reasoning, and of intense and continued application.[8]

Unfortunately, he didn't stop there. Gisborne goes on to say these qualities should only be "imparted to the female mind with a more sparing hand" and continues by describing the female mind and its strengths, which by no surprise, happen to align with the sanctioned roles for women during his time: get pregnant, have children, take care of husband and children till death do you part.

Fast-forward 200 years, and we see the "updated" version written by Cambridge University psychologist Simon Baron-Cohen.

"The female brain is predominantly hard-wired for empathy. The male brain is predominantly hard-wired for understanding and building systems."[9]

He thereby draws the conclusion men make the best scientists, lawyers, bankers, and engineers. Of course, you know what's coming when he enlightens us as to which professions the female brain is best suited for. That's right: counselors, primary school teachers, nurses, social workers, personnel staff, and therapists. So are we to glean from this that women couldn't possibly have enough brainpower to teach the more challenging years of study beginning in about the seventh or eighth grade?

Fine shares several studies in her book that demonstrate test result differences when gender is primed—that is, participants are reminded of their gender just before the test.

In one study, French high school students were asked to comment on how true gender stereotypes are as they relate to math and arts aptitude. Following this question, they were then asked to rate their own ability in each of these areas.[10] The students had taken a national standardized test two years prior, so they were to report on their performance on this test. The control group participants were not primed with the gender stereotype question before reporting their test results.

The girls, primed with the gender stereotype question, rated themselves higher in the arts than they had actually scored and lower in math than their actual performance, as compared to the control group. The boys, primed with gender stereotypes, did the opposite. They rated themselves higher in math than they had actually performed and lower in art than their actual performance, as compared to the control group.

Fine also notes in studies, checking a female or male box before taking a test has been proven to alter results.[11] What wires gender, according to Fine, is our minds, society, and neurosexism, a term she coined herself that describes "science" that has historically justified the gender stereotypes of its time.

In a 2017 article written by Gina Rippon, "How 'Neurosexism' is Holding Back Gender Equality—and Science Itself," Rippon defines neurosexism as follows:

"Neurosexism is the practice of claiming that there are fixed differences between female and male brains, which can explain women's inferiority or unsuitability for certain roles."[12]

Our general understanding is growing that the traits we think of as female or male exist on a spectrum and that behavioral characteristics do not fall into two nice and neat, mutually exclusive categories. For example, we are seeing men's advantage and strength in spatial cognition—the understanding of spatial environments, angles, directions, and distance—diminishing and even disappearing. In some cultures, it is reversed, and women are showing a spatial ability advantage due to advanced education and increased opportunities.[13]

The notion of a "female" and "male" brain, one better than the other for certain professions and skillsets, has shown to be flawed in current studies. Think it has anything to do with the inroads we are making to provide equal access to education; to socially, intellectually, and creative toys; and to equal opportunities for our kids, regardless of gender identity?

Mahzarin Banaji, a Harvard University psychologist, nails it when she said, "There isn't a bright line separating self from culture," and "Culture has a very deep reach into our minds." Male domination and male supremacy have been reinforced and justified in all corners of the world, in just about every field of study, and continue to drive national agendas, one country after another.

While living in St. Louis, I attended countless meetings to end sexism and racism, support immigrants, and organize peace initiatives. I noticed that one of the women's social justice organizations had many events on racism but almost nothing about sexism and the violence women endure. How could this be? How can women not make the epidemic rates of male violence committed against women a top priority when women are on the front lines of just about every other social justice issue?

I reached out to the leader of the group and her response was "there is nothing new" in the area of domestic violence. Really? Nothing new. Every day three women are murdered by an intimate partner, every nine seconds a woman is beaten, and every six minutes a woman is raped. Tell that to the families who lost their daughter, or the children of the mother who was murdered, or the grandparents who had to bury not only their daughter but their grandchildren as well.

At a 2019 town hall meeting in Charleston, South Carolina, Kamala Harris talked about violence against black males three times, and not once did she mention the violence against black women—or women at all for that matter—other than in her opening remarks, when she did include sexism and racism as ills in the country.

In one of the debates with Hillary Clinton during the 2016 election, Bernie Sanders said reproductive rights are a distraction. Clinton's response? Not to millions of women it's not. When asked about the pay disparity between women and men working on his 2016 campaign, Sanders remarked that he had been pretty busy with the campaign traveling across the country. Perhaps it is understandable not to be aware of all the details, yet given his response, it didn't seem important when it was brought to his attention.

While at the library in 2019 looking through new nonfiction books, I came across one written by two male authors discussing the emotional well-being of college students, their anxieties, and how college plays a key role. The authors listed the top news stories related to social justice between 2009 and 2018. They cited specific men's names approximately twenty times, whereas only two women were cited—Caitlyn Jenner, trans female, and Heather Heyer, who was killed by a neo-Nazi at a protest in Charlottesville, Virginia.

Only two women were cited as newsworthy in the arena of social justice during a ten-year period and one of them because of her death? This brought back painful memories of the labor-intensive research I did years ago, poring over St. Louis newspapers, to look at how often and where women were featured on the front pages of major sections of the newspapers. It was rare to see a woman above the newspaper fold, and if there was a story that featured a woman on the front page, it was most likely because she had been murdered and/or raped. Close to twenty years have passed since my newspaper research, yet the featured stories, back then and now, were about the same.

In the book about the emotional well-being of college students, I counted thirteen citings of racism but only as it affected black men, sexism two times with a reference to the #MeToo movement and the 2017 Women's March, and LGBTQ+-related issues about five times. These are all interrelated of course and important, yet of all social justice issues listed, just two women cited. With 51 percent of the population being female, how could that be?

Kamala Harris, Bernie Sanders, social justice organization leaders, and the authors of the book cited previously, are like most of us. We have biases and blind spots, conditioned to tune out the contributions, the inequalities, and resulting struggles—including the violence—that befall women.

When the fabric, the privilege, and lack thereof, by which we have come to be, is based on human constructs, it becomes a self-fulfilling prophecy, and we all play roles in its perpetuation. Fortunately, we play equally important roles in the solution, and that means there is a lot of muscle available to move forward in a more fair and just way.

It's important to avoid the blame-and-shame model because we're all in on this, on the perpetuation of inequality. In some way, we are all plugging into it, which is also the good news. It means we can unplug and become the solution.

It was Steve Biko, the South African anti-apartheid activist, who brilliantly pointed out, "The most potent weapon in the hands of the oppressor is the mind of the oppressed."[14]

Is it this mindset that had so many women vote for a man to be a U.S. president, who not only admitted he sexually assaults women but also bragged about it? Could it be because it protected "white men at the helm" world order as they know it, along with their husbands' jobs and the lives they were living?

Is it the mindset of oppressed women that has them speak out about racially motivated violence committed by police officers yet stay silent when violence in the home is present?

And what about the mindset of the oppressor? Here are some examples, in the early 1900s, of men who fought to protect their privileges, keeping women from the voting booth. These are statements made by Members of the British Parliament in the early 1900s from the House of Commons records.

> Men have the vote and the power at the present moment; I say for Heaven's sake let us keep it. We are controlled and worried enough by women at the present time, and I have heard no reason why we should alter the present state of affairs.
>
> **—Sir James Grant, MP for Whitehaven**

> There are obvious disadvantages about having women in Parliament. I do not know what is going to be done about their hats. How is a poor little man to get on with a couple of women wearing enormous hats in front of him?
>
> **—Rowland Hunt, MP for Ludlow**

> You have at the present moment certain statistics which show that both the birth and marriage rate are decreasing. Can you adopt

at this time a policy which might mean an immense destruction of the population of the country which it is essential should not only be retained, but increased.

**—Sir Charles Hobhouse, MP for Bristol East
and Chancellor of the Duchy of Lancaster**

Intuition is far more largely developed in women than in men, but instinct and intuition, although good guides, are not the best masters so far as Parliament is concerned. Parliament exists for the very purpose of opposing feelings, fancies, and inclinations by reason.

—Godfrey Collins, MP for Greenock

And in a U.S. pamphlet distributed in 1910 by the National Association Opposed to Woman Suffrage—they gave us these "highly intelligent stories":

BECAUSE 90 percent of the women either do not want it, or *do not care.*

BECAUSE it means *competition* of women with men instead of *cooperation.*

BECAUSE 80 percent of the women eligible to vote are married and can only double or annul their husband's votes.

BECAUSE it can be of no benefit commensurate with the additional expense involved.

BECAUSE in some states more voting women than voting men will place the government under petticoat rule.

BECAUSE it is unwise to risk the good we already have for the evil that may occur.

And *"You do not need a ballot to clean out your sink spout."*

Although perhaps somewhat humorous today, these were the "stories" of a not-too-distant era and reasons to hold women back. Every generation has them, including the present day.

It is time to be intentional in our work and in our conversations to more accurately recognize, respect, honor, and reflect the true diversity of contributions made within our communities, nations, and the world.

Imagine a world that does that. Now those are stories worth telling.

Part Two

Our Responsibility—Our Time

*With the new day comes new strength and
new thoughts.*

—Eleanor Roosevelt

SIX

The Shift: From Habits of Inequality to Habits of Equality

The way to right wrongs is to turn the light of truth upon them.

—Ida B. Wells-Barnett

Habits—they get a hold on us, for good or for bad. The English poet John Dryden put it this way:

We first make our habits and then our habits make us.

In my work as a coach over the last twenty years, I have supported my clients to learn and live habits of health, replacing habits of disease. Put the good habits in place, and you will naturally crowd out the not-so-good habits. It is the way to a healthier, longer life. It's pretty simple stuff with a huge payoff.

Habits of health include the following:

1. Breakfast within thirty to sixty minutes of getting up
2. Small-portion, nutrient-dense meals every two to three hours, mostly plant foods
3. About sixty-four ounces of water every day
4. At least seven hours of sleep each night
5. Stress reduction throughout the day
6. Physical activity most days of the week

Habits of disease are the opposite:

1. Not eating breakfast within thirty to sixty minutes of getting up
2. Not eating nutrient-dense meals (mostly plant food) throughout the day
3. Little water
4. Little sleep
5. Not managing stress/emotions throughout the day
6. Little or no physical activity

Look at the health of the United States, with its growing population of obese children and adults, skyrocketing sick-care costs, and alarming rates of addiction, depression, dementia, type 2 diabetes, and heart disease. It is pretty clear we are living more habits of disease than habits of health.

> The U.S. ranked last on performance overall and ranked last or near last on the Access, Administrative Efficiency, Equity, and Health Care Outcomes domains. The top-ranked countries overall were the U.K., Australia, and the Netherlands. Based on a broad range of indicators, the U.S. health system is an outlier, spending far more but falling short of the performance achieved by other high-income countries.[1]

Of eleven nations studied in the Commonwealth Fund report (Australia, Canada, France, Germany, the Netherlands, New Zealand, Norway, Sweden, Switzerland, the United Kingdom, and the United States), the United States ranks last, as it did in the 2017, 2014, 2010, 2007, 2006, and 2004 editions of *Mirror, Mirror*.[2]

And where do you go from dead last?

Well, we can keep doing what we're doing, and while we're doing it, we will most likely incur greater sick-care costs, more medications and doctor visits, a greater likelihood of costly and preventable illness and disease, and premature death.

There is, of course, another option.

Add one habit of health at a time (or more if so inclined), and your body will reward you with better health, a healthier weight, higher energy, fewer sick days, lower sick-care costs, and a better quality of life. Not only does an individual get healthier, but also so does a nation and a world. In other words, we all win as each of us gets healthier, living habits of health.

For more than a decade I have listened to people share their health status with me. One of the things they talk about is their family history.

"It runs in the family."

"My mother and grandmother died of heart attacks."

"There is a lot of type 2 diabetes in my family."

Fortunately, I hear this less and less. Today, I more often hear, "I know I need to change what I'm doing. I can't seem to make the changes stick." Or, "I know what to do; I just don't do it."

This represents a powerful shift in a person's life and the health of their family. This level of self-awareness and acknowledgment of personal responsibility can begin a journey back to great health.

So how does a discussion about health fit in with a book about equality and peace? Well, I also hear this a lot:

"It's tradition."

"We've always done it that way."

"It's in the Bible."

"It's the holiday."

"It's what you do at a wedding."

"They're old-fashioned."

Sound familiar?

As we are learning to take more responsibility for our health, connecting the dots from the daily cheeseburger and French fries to the heart medication, insulin, and expanding waistline, so we must with the choices we make, and the beliefs and traditions we live, that perpetuate inequality.

Only when we make different choices will we get different results. Because the disease or tradition runs in the family doesn't mean it must continue to do so. The scale tips toward equality, nation by nation, as individuals live the habits that favor, promote, and uphold equality and equal access to opportunities and resources.

Look what happens as we level the playing field and women take their rightful place in industry, government, and health care.

Highest representation of women executives and corporate board members yields higher rates of return.

- 35% higher return on equity and 34% higher total return to shareholders for 353 Fortune 500 companies with the highest representation of women in senior leadership roles.[3]

- 15% increase in profits for companies with leadership teams that are minimally 30% female.[4]

▸ 74% higher return on assets and equity for the twenty-five California companies with the highest percentage of women executives and board members. This study included William-Sonoma, Yahoo, and Wells Fargo.[5]

Female legislators legislate more.[6]

▸ Congresswomen pass an average of 2.31 bills versus 1.57 for Congressmen.

▸ Congresswomen obtain 9% more money for their districts, amounting to $49 million annually.

Women doctors achieve better outcomes.[7]

▸ Fewer patients die, have complications 30 days following surgery, or are readmitted to the hospital with female surgeons.

▸ A Harvard study of more than 1.5 million hospitalized Medicare patients had lower 30-day mortality and lower 30-day hospital readmissions with female internists.

Peace accords last longer when women are part of the process.

▸ Peace is 35% more likely to last at least fifteen years when women are part of peace negotiations.[8]

▸ In a study that looked at forty-two armed conflicts and eighty-two peace agreements between 1989 and 2011, "durable peace" was more likely when women were part of the peace process.[9]

The more diverse the company and teams of leaders, the better we become, and the better off we are. Why do I believe this to be the case? Here's one more study before we get to that.

Christina Boedker, of the Australian School of Business, conducted a study among 5,600 people within seventy-seven organizations to see if there was a correlation between leadership and organizational performance. She found that the leader's ability to be empathetic and compassionate had the greatest impact on organizational profitability and productivity.[10]

Empathetic and compassionate.

So, back to the question, why is diversity key to better results?

When it comes to gender identity, we raise "females" and "males" differently, as has been discussed, and treat those who identify as female or male differently throughout a lifetime. Although this is a broad generalization and doesn't apply to every family, every parent, every child, and every person, it is highly prevalent in U.S. society and societies across the globe.

There are two fundamental differences in how females and males are traditionally raised that can significantly affect one's mindset, skill set, and abilities.

1. **Unequal access to the full range of human emotions and feelings and comfort in expressing one's emotions and feelings.**

   - Females: greater access and greater comfort

   - Males: less access and less comfort

2. **Different definitions of what success in life is.**

   - Females: connections/relationships, love, compassion, collaboration

• Males: money, competition, winning, power

Each of these paths creates different mindsets, skill sets, and abilities. Add into the mix a patriarchal society, and you have those with less emotional awareness (self-awareness and social awareness), resilience, and coping skills, plus an identity based on money and power, along with a sense of entitlement, running the show. On the flip side of the coin, you have those with greater emotional awareness (self-awareness and social awareness), resilience, and coping skills, with an identity based on relationships, collaboration, and compassion, with less power and access to resources and opportunities.

My mother and father, together, created the optimal environment for our family. Without my mother, the intimate connections, level of care, compassion, and empathy were not the same. We can see it in businesses and governments where the bottom line is more about money than the state of the environment, children, education, health, and happiness.

Each of us, regardless of our gender identity, has the same ability to love, be compassionate, and empathize when we do not get in the way. It is a matter of raising our children with this as our desired outcome, and supporting one another through adulthood to choose one's own path, rather than as gendered individuals with a prescribed role in life, based on outdated norms and traditions.

I will add, at this point, that diversity across the board is vitally important. Diversity by gender, race, nationality, religion, age, physical abilities, sexual orientation, and socioeconomic status is key to creating solutions best for all concerned and the only way to do so.

So let's take a closer look at how this plays out in norms, long-standing beliefs, and traditions that perpetuate gender-based double standards, which I call habits of inequality. Just as habits of disease create disease, habits of inequality give us disease in the form of poverty, conflict, violence, greed, corruption, damage to the environment, and war. As we eliminate inequality, we create the space for people to rise to their full potential without conflict. From that place, the challenges before us can be overcome.

Here are some examples of habits of inequality that perpetuate gender inequality and the persistent gender gap.

Pink for Girls, Blue for Boys

I can't count the number of times I have gone into a toy store and was asked, "Are you shopping for a girl or a boy?" My response was always pretty much the same. I'd inform the person that I was shopping for a child, give their age, and usually add that gender was irrelevant.

Here are some coloring books I recently came across:

The Beautiful Girls Colouring Book (pink cover with butterflies, flowers, cakes, and animals) and *The Brilliant Boys Colouring Book* (blue cover with space machines, helmets, and axes).

Ouch. Imagine, females of the world, you are sitting next to your brother, and he's coloring in the *Brilliant Boys Coloring Book*, and you are coloring in the *Beautiful Girls Coloring Book*. Can you see the two starkly different trajectories of life playing out from there? Can you also connect the dots from each of these paths to examples of gender inequality we experience today? Crystal clear, I hope.

Children are ascribed to two different worlds based on an assigned gender at birth. I am not suggesting there is anything inherently wrong with the colors pink or blue or books about princesses or kitchen sets. It is the assignment of one or the other, based on biology, that makes no sense and is inequitable.

It is kind of like deciding a child's profession at childhood, the college they will go to, what they will study, the sports they will play, and on and on—all at birth.

How many girls will see themselves in their princess books and costumes creating the next groundbreaking, hi-tech invention or scoring the winning run? How many boys will dance, or teach, or strive to be the best dad they can be with the thousands of messages they will receive to win at all costs, that feelings are for sissies, and that physical force makes heroes?

Pink and blue are colors, kitchen sets and Legos are toys, and babies have no concept of any of them until we give the concepts to them. Just as you don't choose colors for your living room or kitchen based on your gender—I haven't seen too many pink kitchens—I suggest you choose colors because you like them and toys that foster social, creative, and intellectual development.

Boys Will Be Boys

This commonly heard phrase sets low expectations for boys and men. It perpetuates entitlement, misconduct, and often illegal acts including rape and other forms of violence.

Too easily dismissed is the poorly behaved little boy, the college football player who gets drunk and rapes a classmate, and the forty-fifth president of the United States who declared during his campaign, "I could stand in the middle of Fifth Avenue and shoot somebody and I wouldn't lose any voters." And let's not forget this same U.S. president's words when he was sixty years old and proclaimed, "And when you're a star, they let you do it. You can do anything. Grab 'em by the pussy. You can do anything."

Remember Brock Turner, a student-athlete attending Stanford University who was found guilty of sexually assaulting an unconscious female student? He was given just six months in jail and served only three months. His father wrote a letter to the court, as did the young woman he assaulted. She outlined in great detail the emotional and physical trauma the assault has caused her.

Brock's father, on the other hand, pleaded with the judge to be lenient on his son. He claimed that night had ruined his son's life and asked the judge not to send his son to prison for "twenty minutes of action." Did this father even consider what his son's "twenty minutes of action" had done to the young woman he assaulted and her family?

Although Brock Turner is rightfully a convicted felon, he is also a victim. He is a victim of society's norms and long-standing beliefs and a victim of traditions that make boys (and sometimes their parents) feel so entitled that rape is a right of passage, making them less responsible for their actions.

Raising our children to believe feelings are for sissies and physical force makes heroes take away their ability to feel another's pain. Combine this with a society that objectifies women's bodies and treats women as collateral damage on the road to manhood, and the "boys will be boys" attitude creates a situation in which there is a reported rape every six minutes. And remember, reported rapes are a small fraction of all rapes committed.

Males do not come out of the womb with this attitude. This stuff is taught, one generation after another, and all of us pay in one way or another. I like to think we can, and that most of us do, raise our children to be, first and foremost, kind and respectful human beings. No gender has a monopoly on kindness and respect nor on responsibility and accountability.

Imagine a world where children are raised with the same expectations regardless of gender, where fair play and collaboration are more important than winning, where power shared rather than power over another is the ultimate goal. Imagine that mindset. Imagine those skills. Imagine that world.

Big Boys Don't Cry

When boys and men are not able to process and manage their emotions and feelings, find comfort in friends and family, and are held to impossible standards of what it means to be a human being, we're creating instability in potentially half of the human species.

"Don't cry." "Man up." "Don't be a sissy." All these are devastating commands to a little boy, and man, in every area of life.

This, in combination with "boys will be boys," is a time bomb waiting to go off. A sense of entitlement plus the lack of access to the full range of human emotions create less resilience and poor coping skills. When things don't go their way, they are ill-equipped to handle it.

A lethal combination is a man who feels shamed, dishonored, a failure in some regard, possibly on the job, financially, or in a relationship. How many times do we hear of a man losing his job or family who violently turns on his coworkers, spouse, and children? It seems like every day.

A study commissioned by Plan International USA and conducted by PerryUndem in 2018, tells us males are still being raised to believe being strong, athletic, and stoic is most important.[11] Boys said being strong and tough were the most valued traits for boys. When they were asked what they did when they felt angry, most of them said they either get aggressive or "just suck it up." When they were afraid, they felt they were expected to hide their feelings and be tough. Females, on the other hand, were more comfortable expressing their emotions, crying, and yelling.

Peaceful and harmonious relationships, with self and others, and resilience, the ability to positively respond to life's challenges no matter what, begin with the ability to feel, process, and express one's own emotions. And feeling, processing, and expressing emotions are all necessary to feel another person's pain and key to a just and fair society.

You may remember that in the leadership study cited earlier conducted by Christina Boedker, of the Australian School of Business, empathy and compassion came out on top. The leader's ability to be empathetic and compassionate had the greatest impact on organizational profitability and productivity. It works for the business, it works for the family, and it works for the individual.

Let's retire "big boys don't cry" once and for all so that big boys and big girls don't die and don't fall prey to violence, depression, drugs, and suicide.

Name-Calling Isn't Nice—In *or* Outside the Sandbox

Name-calling can be as common as a cup of coffee in the morning and as habit-forming. Historian Gerda Lerner said, "The vilest insults in every language refer to parts of the female body or to female sexuality." Lerner tells us that women will never be taken seriously until we stop allowing our language to "define and degrade" us in such a manner.[12]

Our language conveys so much about us. Individually, name-calling conveys our own fears, biases, and prejudices. Collectively, it conveys how pervasive prejudice and fear are throughout society.

Name-calling is something we teach our children not to do, yet as a culture, it has become widely accepted and can be heard far too frequently coming out of the mouths of elected leaders. Large groups of people justify it on a daily basis. In the mix, are so many derogatory names for women, that it's difficult to keep up with all of them.

Witch, dame, battleaxe, chick, girl, arm candy, dog, bag, bitch, broad, cunt, slut, girly, hussy, trollop, slag, vixen, wench.

More neutral words are oftentimes used with the intention to degrade or diminish women. For example, men call other men "ladies" or refer to female characteristics and practices in a diminishing way. In movies, you'll often hear male police officers and drill sergeants yell out, "Welcome ladies!" or coaches when the team is losing or made a bad play, "Listen up ladies!" I suppose some like to think women are weak so they can feel strong. But name-calling and putting others down to feel better about yourself are signs of weakness.

I'd like to ask those men if they've experienced childbirth, if they've seen Serena Williams hit a tennis ball, or Sarah Thomas, the first person to swim the English Channel four times nonstop, or the U.S. Women's Soccer team. And what about all the assaults women endure, the daily harassment on the street and in the office, all while mothering their children—one of the most demanding roles of all, while pursuing degrees and careers? There's nothing weak about any of that.

Unfortunately, not only is name-calling part of conversations among "the guys," but they can be heard among "the gals" as well. Women have also been socialized to join in on their own degradation.

When we insult girls and women in the process of making a point of any kind, in a song, movie, or otherwise, we perpetuate discrimination, violence, and gender inequality. We are all part of the same human team, and teams don't put each other down and then expect to go out and win the game. Neither can we.

In every day, there are 1,440 minutes. That means we have 1,440 daily opportunities to make a positive impact.

—Les Brown

We have so many opportunities to make a positive impact each and every day. Let's not use them up with name-calling, which does so much harm.

Calling Women Girls

This one has women get more defensive than just about any other gender-based norm we live with today. I got it: you don't mind, you think it's cute, it's endearing, and makes you feel young. After all, there's no real harm, is there? I only ask that you hang in there with me to understand why it is harmful to us all.

We typically refer to men as boys only when we are calling out childish behavior. We're suggesting he is acting childish and immature when we call him a boy. Women are called girls by women and men alike, regardless of age and behavior, all the time—another norm, another habit of inequality.

Whether you are twenty or sixty-five, if you're female, people will refer to you as a girl. She's forty years old, and she's a salesgirl. She's a fifty-year-old vice president and still referred to as a girl.

Yet who calls a fifty-year-old man a salesboy? Who calls the male vice president a boy? As a matter of fact, type in *salesgirl* in Microsoft Word, and it comes up as a word; there's no red squiggly line under it. Type in *salesboy,* and it comes up as an error with a red squiggly underline, letting us know it is not a word.

So regardless of age or title, men are men at adulthood, clear and simple, yet women remain girls for life. If we want to be paid like an adult and treated equally, then we'd better get uncomfortable being called children.

African American men do not accept being called boy because they know they deserve the respect of any other man. Hearing the word boy when referring to an African American man growing up in the sixties was chilling. It's the same chill I get today every time I hear a woman called a girl when in the same scenario the male in the room is called a man.

Dr. Martin Luther King Jr. shared a story from his childhood when he and his father were driving one day and a police officer pulled up alongside their car. The officer told Dr. King's father to pull over and called him a boy in the process. Dr. King's father explained to the officer that his son was a boy and that he was a man, and unless he referred to him accordingly, he would not pull over.[13]

It is a double standard women themselves uphold when in one breath they say, "No I would never call an African American man a boy" and at the same time, "I don't mind being called a girl. It's no big deal."

There it is, the mindset of the oppressed that has a woman say she wants a man for a life partner, not a boy, while referring and thinking of herself as a girl. We made the switch from fireman to firefighter, chairman to chairperson, Congressman to Congressperson; we can do the same here.

To be clear, I'm not talking about slang expressions like "girls night out" or "hanging out with the boys," or "go girl," and so on. These are expressions that are equally used and bring with them our playful sides and child-like spirit. I'm not referring to these.

What I am referring to are the countless times per week I am in groups with adults and I hear someone say, "the girl that owns the consulting business" or "the girl who wrote the article." I'm yet to hear a woman or a man say "the boy who owns the consulting firm" or "the boy partner in the law firm."

I did an internet search for "girl" and "boy" using Google and got this:

- "A girl is a female human from birth through childhood and adolescence to attainment of adulthood when she becomes a woman. The term girl may also be used to mean *a young woman*."

- "A boy is a young male human, usually a child or adolescent. When he becomes an adult, he is described as a man. Commonly applies to adult men, either considered in some way *immature or inferior*."

If you still doubt this is a big deal, as many women do, I suggest you start calling men, presidents of companies and countries, "boy," and see how it feels. If we accept it for one and not the other, that's a double standard, a habit of inequality, with serious consequences.

In some households, girls are given less allowance, and in most companies, women are paid, on average, 20 percent less for the same work a man does. In the United States, it takes some time in April of the following year for a woman to make what a man does in the prior twelve months.

Men often use the expression, "man up." It's time for women to "woman up" and stop letting anyone refer to them as a child. And remember, children need guidance, adult supervision, and if women are girls/children, then that guidance must come from men.

The mindset creates the world we live in. Shifting this one will transform the world and why I named this book *Call Me a Woman*.

Remember, U.S. founding documents do not say "all boys are created equal." Perhaps when women understand this, as African American men did, we will get our amendment too.

Females Subsumed in the Male Pronoun

Another wonderful quote from historian Gerda Lerner is:

> We women have had to express ourselves through patriarchal thought as reflected in the very language we have had to use. It is a language in which women are subsumed under the male pronoun and in which the generic term for human is male.[14]

Oh boy. Oh man. Mankind. Manpower. Chairman. Fireman. Policeman. Freshman. Man the fort. Man the ship. Airman. Parents talking to their children using "he" when referring to every animal at the zoo or in the picture book. "C as in Charlie, V as in Victor, B as in boy." I always follow when people on the phone do that with, "You can use female names also. That would be nice and inclusive."

It's been a long time since women in the United States were denied an education, the opportunity to serve in the military, and leadership in an organization. It's time to shift our language to reflect reality and the more equal and inclusive society we want to create. And as we do so, as we change our language to reflect inclusion and equality, we change hearts and minds. We also change our destiny.

Not that long ago, I heard a man at an art fair tell his wife to man the booth. I said, "She can't. She can woman the booth, but she can't man it." He totally lost it. I asked him if it would be okay to ask him to woman the booth. That didn't go over well either. Clearly, this can be serious stuff, challenging male entitlement, even when it comes to accurately using the language.

Interestingly, when "men" was used in the founding documents of the United States, they did mean men only—one of the few places the word was used accurately.

Our language expresses both values and norms. Male preference in our language is a precursor to male privilege elsewhere, in the recording of news and history, on the job, in the interviewing process, hiring, compensation, and elections. Language is powerful. Let's use it to create the world we want.

Women Subsumed in Marriage

Few institutions are more rife with habits of inequality than marriage. From the engagement to the marriage ceremony, there are so many norms and traditions that seem as though they could only have existed until the early twentieth century, not the early twenty-first. Let's take a look.

Starting out on a positive note, the *BRIDES* 2016 American Wedding Study lets us know a significant number of couples today, 73 percent, are paying for the entire wedding themselves or a portion of it rather than the long-standing tradition of the bride's family paying for the wedding.[15] This long-held tradition of the bride's family paying for the wedding is on its way out. Today's couples and their families are sharing the costs more and more.

However, women are still waiting to be asked out, waiting for the proposal, and some even waiting for him to ask her father or parents if he can marry her. I read in an otherwise seemingly progressive woman's Facebook post how cute she thought it was that her boyfriend asked her dad for his permission to marry her. All I could think was, *wow*.

Being handed off from one man to another was the custom in the 1800s, when women had virtually no rights. A woman's status depended upon being married, hence the phrase "old maid." What's the male counterpart to an old maid? Well of course there is none, for it is the man who decides when and if he marries, and society holds him of equal value regardless of his marital status.

That's not the case for women, as can be seen at a typical wedding. Mom usually sits on the sidelines as dad and daughter walk down the aisle before the handoff. If dad is not in the picture, I've heard women say, "Oh, who will give me away?"

"Give me away?" Please think about the mindset that normalizes this statement. Would you allow this in any other context, one person giving another person away? It's unheard of until it comes to females entering into a marriage.

He's a groomsman and she's a bridesmaid. If she's married she's a matron of honor. Women are maids or matrons, whereas men remain men.

"You may now kiss the bride." Interesting how all of a sudden the wedding switches to "you," and the "you" means "him," putting the woman, once again, in the position of waiting to be acted upon. That one always hurts. I long for the wedding when I hear, "You may now kiss the groom" or "You may now kiss one another."

"I now pronounce you man and wife." Again, he stays a person—a man—and she becomes a role—a wife. I'm hearing this less and less, thank goodness.

"Let me be the first to introduce Mr. and Mrs. John Smith." This is one of the worst. She is reduced to Mrs., her name completely wiped out. Now all that is left of her is her marital status. Women were granted the right to own property over one hundred years ago, yet still can't hold onto their names, in some cases, not even their first names. In 1847, Elizabeth Cady Stanton wrote, "The custom of calling women Mrs. John This and Mrs. Tom That . . . is founded on the principle that white men are lords of all."

Liz Susong, editor of Catalyst Wedding Co., points out that we can take a few lessons from queer and same-sex couples on how to begin a marriage on more equal footing.[16] She writes, "Some same-sex couples understand the tradition of one person taking the other's last name to be rooted in a patriarchal, property-based history of marriage, in which a woman is subservient to her husband, and they, therefore, want zero part of that." She cites one woman who said, "We both loved our names and adamantly did not want to change them."

Another woman Susong cites, in a same-sex marriage, put it this way: "We didn't want to just recycle the tradition of the woman taking the man's name since there is no man here, no one is anyone's property, and sadly, no goats were exchanged during this process. Marriage is the intertwining of two lives, and we even wanted to intertwine our names."

Susong tells us some queer and same-sex couples will combine their last names and create a new last name, hyphenate the two names, or choose one or the other based on family history—or they simply prefer one name over the other.

Women have been taught from the start to subordinate themselves, and apparently, heterosexual marriage is not the occasion to disrupt this gender-based practice, not even for young women. The slightly good news is the number of women keeping their original names is up from 17 percent in the 1970s to 20 percent in 2020, based on a Google Consumer Survey.[17] However, this is still a small percentage opting out of this long-standing habit of inequality.

Imagine two young people, one female and one male, graduating law school. They decide to become partners and start a law practice. Imagine it is common practice that his name only goes on the shingle, so Smith and Associates on the front of the building it is. He is Smith and she is part of the Associates. Just like "Mrs. John Smith" says she's there—kind of.

Would you appreciate your name or your daughter's name not being part of the firm's name, one of the two founding partners, after all that education and hard work? Most likely not. So why do we go along with this, usually without any conversation, for the family name, just assuming she will be the one to give up hers?

This next one is even tougher for most women to get their heads around, even those who did not change their names when they got married.

"Why do your children have his last name only and not yours?" I ask them.

"Well, because that's my husband's last name."

"Well, yes, but what about your family name?"

Then when they realize where I'm going, I often hear, "Well, how would that be fair to him?" Exactly, which begs the question: well, how is it fair to you? Then it's usually something like, "Oh that doesn't bother me" or "I never liked my last name." Interesting how I've never heard a man claim he didn't like his last name so he changed it to his wife's last name. We defend our choices ruthlessly, even when it means our self-disempowerment.

And we're right back to "that's how it's always been done" or "it's tradition." It's a good thing abolitionists and current-day civil rights activists never accepted slavery and racism in the same way, "Well, it's tradition or the way it's been done for hundreds of years." Women have long held up the patriarchy by succumbing, generation after generation, to self-imposed inequalities.

The marriage, the way we begin our families, is an important modeling moment for the relationship and for our children. If we could connect the dots, perhaps we would see other concessions women feel they must make and men expect because now they are "man and wife" or "Mr. and Mrs. John Smith."

Gerda Lerner one more time: "Women, more than any other group, have collaborated in their own subordination through their acceptance of the sex-gender system. They have internalized the values that subordinate them to such an extent they voluntarily pass them on to their children."[18]

We can legislate equal pay, safety for women, and equal rights all day long, yet if we continue to live these antiquated habits of inequality as we begin our families, what hope do we have for future generations to do it any differently?

"Miss and Mrs."

Several years ago I challenged my local chamber of commerce as they expected women to choose on the application whether they were Mrs., Miss, or Ms. I'm still stunned today that women are being asked this archaic question and answering it.

I told them I could not rejoin the chamber if I were discriminated against in this manner. If men are not expected to declare their marital status to join the chamber or any other organization, then women should not be.

Again, we must understand where this comes from and that its time has come and gone, as much as women not voting or owning property has come and gone. I was pleased to see a year or so later they did change the form and eliminated the Miss and Mrs. checkboxes.

One more story may hopefully drive a final nail in this coffin. I remember watching a top-rated TV show on Netflix and one male detective called another male detective, whose partner was female, Mrs., and her last name. Again, she was the male detective's boss. The inference was that he was weak and controlled by a woman. How unmanly that was.

Yet it is not considered "unwomanly" when women are called Mrs. Smith (his last name) or Mrs. John Smith. This is because being "womanly" is to be dominated by men, give up one's name at marriage, be subsumed in male pronouns, and on and on. We must notice these double standards for what they are—habits of inequality, marginalizing women, and keeping the status quo in place.

"The Man of the House"

From time to time I still hear this in a movie or TV show. It's said to the son after the father has gone or died, "You're the man of the house now." We all know what the implication is here. He's now in charge. Woman of the house? I've never heard that said to a daughter, implying a position of power.

"Who wears the pants in this family?" is the same sort of thing. These are expressions that fortunately are going by the wayside. Let's keep them going in that direction.

"She Doesn't Work"

It is said that two-thirds of the world's work is done by women, much of it unpaid. It's time we honor the work women do. I encourage women never to say "I'm just a housewife" or "I don't work." If you care for the home and children, you most likely work as many hours as those who work outside the home—in many cases more.

Breaking News: Ovaries Are Not Required for Housework

Women, on average, do more housework than men, even when they work full time outside the home. Even when she has the "bigger job" and earns more money, she comes home and does more housework than her male partner does. In Japan, women who work outside the home still do twenty-five hours a week of housework, whereas their husbands do less than five.[19]

In Britain, women do 60 percent more unpaid work than men.[20] In Sweden, where they do a much better job in terms of gender equality than most countries, women spend forty-five minutes more per day on housework.[21] Heterosexual couples could learn a thing or two from same-sex couples about sharing the workload at home. Studies show same-sex couples are much better at sharing the workload with some chores divided up by preference and some shared.[22]

Francine Deutsch, author of *Halving It All*, tells the story of two couples. In the one couple, she was a college professor, and he was a physician. In the other, she was the physician, and he was the college professor. The women and men in both couples said the man's job was less flexible.

Cordelia Fine, once again from the book *Delusions of Gender*, says it this way, "But it is curious just how bendy and stretchy a woman can make a job that appears to be a good deal more rigid and inflexible when pursued by a male."[23]

I experienced this myself. My daughter's father was a commercial electrician, and I was a vice president. I made my job bend in every direction I could. I remember one summer picking my daughter up midday from her summer camp and taking her home, then heading back to the office to finish my day. It took about two hours over my "lunch hour" to make that trip daily for the many weeks of her camp. On business trips, I would make numerous calls to research schools, summer camps, and doctors. I look back at this and see it was a choice I made and one many other women do as well. For that, I'd like a do-over.

I learned the hard way the truth of Gloria Steinem's statement, "Women are not going to be equal outside the home until men are equal in it."

I could have done a much better job of equalizing the home front with a weekly family discussion about what needs to be done for the upcoming week. Speaking up for myself would only have required one simple statement, "Let's talk about how we can divide this up."

Given more dolls and kitchen sets than creative and intellectual toys, and the many gender-based messages females and males receive growing up, the line in the sand has been difficult to wash away. Women continue to do most of the caregiving and housework. The impact is huge as it leads to many women deciding their job is less important than his. After all, his salary has grown while hers has not, given all the adjustments she has made to her job to accommodate family care.

Only when fathers are equal parents to their
children will women truly be free.
—**Justice Ruth Bader Ginsburg**

Can't Find Women in Your History Books?

As we've established, it's because they are barely there.

I hope by now it's clear how important this piece of the mosaic is in achieving equality. How we view ourselves is critical to reaching our full potential.

When one-half of the population does not see themselves in history books, quotes, street signs, and holidays on calendars, the most highly revered places in a culture, you can't help but create many people who feel limited in their potential. They will hold themselves back, not take charge, or be the first to speak out when in many instances they are exactly the right person to do so.

How about the Movies?

According to the Geena Benchmark Report 2007–2017, conducted by the Geena Davis Institute on Gender in Media, we are inching our way to greater diversity on the big screen.[24] Over twenty years the institute has created the largest body of research on the subject.

This study is important because we know what we see in movies, TV, and newspapers gives us a glimpse into what a culture deems most valuable and shapes our view of ourselves and our place in the world. When we see mostly heterosexual white men without disabilities, that's an important message to children. They learn that everybody else matters less.

Here are the study's results:

▸ Male leads outnumber female leads two to one; this has improved slightly over the past ten years.

- Family movies that have female leads are now the top earners, earning more than family movies with male leads.

- White leads outnumber leads featuring people of color four to one.

- Revenues from family movies with diverse casts have now caught up with family movies with white leads.

- Less than 1 percent of family movies feature a lead who is LGBTQ+, and there has been no progress here in the past ten years.

- Less than 1 percent of movies feature a lead with a disability, and there has been no progress here in the past ten years.

Boys and men are used to seeing themselves in positions of power, dominating others in almost all areas of life. This feeling is reinforced in the movie industry as well as TV. Good news for all of us is we are seeing some changes within the industry to better depict the diverse world we live in.

GLAAD (formerly the Gay and Lesbian Alliance Against Defamation) is a media-monitoring organization founded in 1985 by LGBTQ+ people and is well-known for tracking the presence of LGBTQ+ characters on TV. GLAAD's *Where We Are on TV* report now includes the number of TV characters by race, gender, and disability.[25]

LGBTQ+ TV characters have increased from 6.4 percent in 2017 to 8.8 percent in 2018. LGBTQ+ characters of color have also increased and now outnumber white LGBTQ+ TV characters. GLAAD has called on the industry to increase the number of LGBTQ+ TV characters to 10 percent within two years.

Although there has been an increase in TV characters with disabilities, it is moving slowly. In 2017, 1.8 percent of TV characters with

disabilities were featured, and in 2018, 2.1 percent of TV characters
with disabilities were featured.

As we see in the Geena Benchmark Report, men far outnumber
women, year by year, in major studio releases. Gay men are more likely
to get the roles in "inclusive" films than gay women. Sixty-four percent
of inclusive films feature gay men. Just 36 percent of inclusive films
feature lesbian characters, according to the 2018 GLAAD report.

Just like girls and women, people with disabilities, LGBTQ+, people
of color, Asian Americans, and so on, are used to not seeing themselves
in TV and in movies, certainly not as leads and in positions of power.
As we hear of greater diversity among writers, as well as those in front
of and behind the camera, we will continue to make progress. Seeing is
believing, and the more diverse the movie industry becomes, the more
empowered, connected, and hopeful people become.

If Looks Could Kill

Although females pursue math, science, and sports for study and careers
in greater numbers than ever before, they are still getting that same old
message that looks matter most. From the same 2018 PerryUndem study
cited earlier, girls do not feel equal when it comes to their bodies.[26] About
75 percent of fourteen- to nineteen-year-olds in the study have felt like
sexual objects or unsafe. They feel society considers physical beauty to
be the most important of all female traits, a view women also share,
according to the study.

Approximately 50 percent of fourteen to nineteen-year-olds and
25 percent of ten to thirteen-year-olds said they hear boys making
sexual comments or jokes on a daily basis. Black and Latino participants are even more likely to hear sexual comments. Eighty-one
percent of girls between the ages of fourteen and nineteen said they
had at least one friend who had been asked by a boy for a naked or
sexy photo.

Women will often do everything they can to look young—Botox, breast enhancements, face-lifts, and hair color, all to cover aging and often at the expense of their own health. If we're not comfortable aging, how can we expect others to be comfortable with our age? Yet I hear women all the time bashing men for being with younger women.

Although the number of older men with young women makes me a bit crazy as well, I remind myself we're all in the same game here. Expectations based on gender lead us to do some pretty insane things. Hoping to defy aging is one of them.

As someone whose mother died at thirty-nine, I treasure the years, and the wrinkles and gray hair feel more like a badge of honor for having endured many ups and downs with amazing lessons learned—lessons I could only have learned with time.

It is time to finish the business of closing the gender gap once and for all. The U.S. Declaration of Independence declared, "We hold these truths to be self-evident, that all men are created equal."

Only men.

It is far beyond time to rewrite the record and right the world. We will do so only as we live lives that reflect the equality we strive for.

SEVEN

The Circle of Life

We don't develop courage by being happy every day.
We develop it by surviving difficult times
and challenging adversity.

—Barbara De Angelis

During a lifetime, we witness extraordinary changes. We tend to think of technology when we think of change from one generation to the next. However, extraordinary changes occur in a generation because of the changes that occur within people.

There are countless examples of those whose lives were greatly restricted or endangered, forced to flee their homes and countries to stay alive and feed their children. Today, their descendants hold postgraduate degrees, are heads of companies, and have become elected officials. Change is inevitable in all realms because we have the ability to change ourselves.

In far too many countries, girls and women are regarded as second-class citizens. Their freedoms are denied and opportunities are restricted. Millions of girls and women are sold into slavery every year, forced to marry as children, genitally mutilated, unequally paid, and unequally represented in about every government across the globe.

On the surface, it appears that men, nation by nation, hold a vast amount of power, or at least more power than women do, and the advantages to keep it that way. The purpose of this book is to look beneath the surface.

The word "holistic" is popular today. We have holistic health care, which focuses on treating the whole person as one system rather than simply addressing a single organ or function. We have holistic education, which focuses on the whole child, where the process the child learns by is as important as facts and formulas—or perhaps more so.

> *The part can never be well unless the whole is well.*
> **—Plato**

As a society we've been moving toward the notion that wholeness is healthy, that viewing a part does not give the whole picture and, in fact, can lead you in the wrong direction. Above all, we are beginning to understand that wholeness means balance, optimal health, and well-being, and the ability not only to sustain oneself but also to thrive.

Picture a circle, full in its wholeness, without beginning or end. Then picture that circle cut in half, still functioning, because enough of it is still intact. But without its other half, it is no longer a circle. If left to stand alone, the one half will always be longing for completion. If the circle has been only half of itself for long enough, it may not know what it's longing for.

And so it goes with human beings. By defining what it means to be a female human being in one way and what it means to be a male human being in another way, with roles to play and specific attributes and values acceptable for one and not the other, we have created extraordinary dysfunction. Neither is whole, which creates unhealthy relationships, dependencies, and self- and societally-imposed limitations on our full potential, our health, and happiness.

Part of being fully human is experiencing all possibilities on the human spectrum. However, if half of the human experience is not available, then that woman—or man—will not have the opportunity to feel balanced or complete. And when an individual doesn't feel balanced or complete—when they sense an essential part of being human is not available to them and they've been so out of touch with it, they don't know what they're missing or yearning for. The result is a world out of balance due to so many of us living imbalanced lives.

Let's talk about men. How are they half of the circle? What is missing in their lives?

Boys are taught, often in subtle ways, even by parents who believe they are raising their girls and boys alike, to be less of a feeling human being than girls. Boys are taught not to cry or to cry less, not to express their true feelings or do so minimally, and often not even to feel their feelings.

A man's man. Wimp. You the man. Don't act like a girl. The list goes on, and these messages are everywhere in society.

Here are two more messages our society sends little boys and girls, moms and dads. Daddy's little girl. Mama's boy. These expressions have conveyed it is okay for a young girl to be connected with her father, but for boys, anything "female-like" is bad, including his own mother!

If boys aren't allowed to feel and express their feelings, to be connected and comforted by family and friends, then what are they to do with those feelings? What are they to do with their disappointment, their anger, anxiety, frustration, overwhelm, sadness, and loneliness? These are feelings whole human beings must feel and process to stay healthy, resilient, successful in life, and fulfilled. Yet, half the population we tell to "stuff it" or else risk not being one of the guys.

We all know what happens far too often when boys and men who are disappointed by life in some way find themselves with a gun in their hands thinking that is the way to prove once and for all they are the man they have been conditioned to become rather than the whole human being they truly are.

Dr. Wayne S. Andersen is the tenth board-certified physician in critical care in the United States, former director of the Surgical Critical Care Program at Grandview Medical Center, *New York Times* bestselling author, and cofounder of Optavia™. I have used this program for a decade to coach my clients to reach a healthy weight and lifestyle. We call it transformation, one healthy habit at a time.

Dr. A, as we call him, is an emotional human being, as are we all. The difference between Dr. A and many men is that he is quite comfortable sharing his emotions. He is filled with passion and purpose for his family and mission to get the world healthy, first as a physician and now a leader in the obesity crisis.

Years ago, speaking at one of our annual conferences with thousands in the audience, Dr. A declared, after an emotional moment and with tears in his eyes, "It's better than picking up an Uzi and shooting people."

To be manly is often understood to be aggressive, and even violent, and to dominate, whether it's on the sports field, a frat house, and far too often at home. Part of being male is to dominate women and part of being female has been to allow it.

It is possible, for both women and men to change all this, despite how society currently defines us. Women have largely redefined their place in society, and continue to do so. Men can do the same.

What if we looked at men in the same way in terms of what is possible for them? What if they were lacking as much as women have been throughout history? It doesn't show up in the external world perhaps—money, career, leadership opportunities. Remember, this is how we raise little boys to measure their success, so this is what we recognize and remember most.

Perhaps freedom for men looks like a world accepting them in their totality: their heart front and center; their feelings felt, expressed, respected, and cared for, and an identity that is based on their ability to love, support, and work alongside others for the greater good.

"Freedom is a constant struggle," said former Atlanta mayor and civil rights leader Andrew Young.

Freedom is also a constant pursuit across the globe and perhaps it starts right here. What if the same opportunities that women have were also available for men? What if my father had been as connected with his emotional self as he was with his drive to succeed externally in the world? What if he had been raised to believe success in life included involvement in his children's lives and their emotional well-being? I'm pretty sure my brother and sisters would remember a different childhood, as would I.

The impact each of us has on another human being is profound. I loved my father beyond words. His kindness, love, humor, and sense of fair play are with me always. We had the best of times, and we had the worst of times. When I think of the worst of times, they stemmed from that lack of connection I believe he had with his own heart, feelings, and emotions.

Even after my mother passed away, Sundays remained a family day for us. Although my father seemed oblivious to the fact his children had not seen him much during the week, and that we also had lives that he might take an interest in, it was the day we were all home together. We learned to participate in his world more than he did ours.

Conversations with my father as a kid were short and surface at best. I can't remember him asking about my life, how school was going, about my grades, friends, what plans I had for college, or even what my plans were for the weekend. I never had a conversation like that with my dad as a child or young adult. Without my mother, it became clear to me, that I was on my own in many ways and that something important in my life was missing.

My mother made a request in the final days of her life. She was thirty-nine years old and aware she was leaving four young children behind. I was told she had asked for three things in her final days, one of which was that my brother, Mark, stay in town and attend Washington University rather than go to college away from home. We joked years later that she made that request because she understood my father was fairly clueless as a parent. A sweet and loving father we certainly had, just not one in tune with the best parenting practices or the notion of reading a book to learn about them.

Mark did stay in town and attended Washington University, honoring my mother and her request. He understood why she asked him to stay and, in turn, was there for us in countless ways, something I am grateful for today. The four of us looked out for each other to make the best of a difficult time in our lives.

Mark went on to become a leader in the biotech industry, as he remains today, as well as cofounder, along with his wife, of an extraordinary nonprofit that supports high school students in learning personal and professional skills for lifelong success. So many kids are going to college that otherwise would not have gone due to their after-school curriculum that uses entrepreneurship as the foundation for learning essential skills needed in the marketplace today. My mother would never know the full impact of that request she made, for him, her daughters, and the world.

I interviewed Mark for this book in 2015 and again in 2019. I wanted to better understand how women are faring in biotech, knowing there is a huge gap between women and men in senior leadership roles, and also to talk about our mother and father and the impact gender had on our lives. They were wonderful conversations.

In the early 1980s when Mark began his career in biotech, there were few women in senior leadership roles, probably less than 5 percent. In

2015, Mark estimated the number was probably closer to 10 to 15 percent. It's still a long way to go, but where Mark went, he made a difference.

When he left as CEO of a large biotech company in Boston, which he also founded several years before, he replaced himself with a woman. I was so proud of him that day and will never forget the call to me when he shared the news. At the time of Mark's departure, seven of the company's most senior leaders were women.

I can't help but think of our mother, knowing in some way she played a role. She was a born leader, and I believe Mark always saw the same possibilities in women as he saw in men because of her. He gives his sisters credit too. We'll take it.

Mark worked with my dad in the shoe stores while attending Washington University to complete both his undergraduate and graduate degrees. He shared with me that he learned how not to manage people based on how my dad managed his employees. With an eighth-grade education, my father did not learn the skills to lead a team and create a strong sense of culture centered on core values. He parented in much the same way, I suppose, without much thought and consideration, more by the seat of his pants, reacting rather than creating.

I'm sure Mark, a voracious reader, took it upon himself to read every book he could on leadership and, when the time came, about parenting. He cited our mother when he said, "I was always aware of what great parenting was because of Mom." Although Mark worked as many hours as my father, just as driven and passionate about his work, he became an involved parent and has a wonderful and rather playful relationship with his daughter.

Mark assures me that biotech is proactive today in bringing women on board; however, there is still a long way to go. These companies, like so many others, now understand that the greater the diversity, the better the company performs. Long-term, Mark told me, the key to closing the leadership gender gap in biotech and technology is building a pipeline of women in science and math who can become the research and development leaders, the CEOs, and the founders of our next generation of companies.

Over the years, Mark made many attempts to diversify biotech. He shared a story with me that began about twenty years ago when he interviewed a woman, a superstar in biotech he called her, with extraordinary accomplishments and experience. In the interview, she told Mark she was not interested in a CEO position, although clearly qualified, because she had young children. Mark was quite surprised when he heard her say those words. Twenty years later he interviewed another female biotech superstar who told him the same thing.

It reminds me of my own proclamation thirty years ago. I had pretty much decided I wanted to be a vice president one day, which I did become, but not a president. With the way most organizations were designed at that time and the way promotions were earned, by working until you drop, you know that next level will require an inordinate amount of time away from a young family. I learned at a young age the importance each of us has in shaping our families. Where there are two parents creating a loving home environment, both are vitally important to a child's whole self-development.

The good news is that more men are feeling this way, too, which means more dads are involved in their children's lives and hopefully taking on an equal share of the workload at home. Companies are becoming more family-friendly today, a win for all of us. And here, too, there is still much work to do.

Both my sisters have also had long, successful careers. Cindy is retired now after years of working in the cancer center for a major Chicago hospital. Cathy is still going strong. Following the elimination of her job during the initial months of COVID-19, and at the age of sixty-two, she co-created a new position with an exciting West Coast company. One of the many things our father taught us lives on. When you get knocked down, you get back up, and oftentimes what you'll find is something far better.

Throughout the many twists and turns, we are a family that remains close, travels together, texts many times during the week, usually about sports and politics, and has raised children that cherish diversity, in all its forms.

I'm so pleased my sisters have maintained our original family name and each of my siblings, as well as my daughter, have chosen wonderful life partners.

Also quite gratifying was watching my father connect more with his feelings and emotions as time went on, even though it was too late to affect our childhoods. I'm reminded of a quote by Eleanor Roosevelt: "As a rule, women know not only what men know but much that men will never know." Fortunately, this is changing, for we know it is not a biological constraint we are bound by. It is a social, human-made construct that need not constrain us any longer.

As a grandfather, my dad attended about every event there was for my daughter. He was struggling later in life with Parkinson's disease, and he still showed up. It meant the world to me and to my daughter. He would always say, "She's special." What I would have given to hear those words from him when I was a young girl.

I cared for my father the last six years of his life and knew he had learned what was most important. He so appreciated me being there and said it often. He'd say, "Laurie, you got the raw end of the deal." I would come back with, "No way, Dad. I got the best gift of all."

Joe Ehrmann, former NFL star, high school football coach, and inspirational speaker, says this of his father: "I think his definition was: Men don't need. Men don't want. Men don't touch. Men don't feel. If you're going to be a man in this world, you better learn how to dominate and control people and circumstances." The scariest words a boy can hear, says Ehrmann, are "be a man."[1]

My father was a remarkable human being in so many ways. Like so many men, he was raised to produce at the expense of deeply connecting—with self and others. We needed and missed that from him as kids. I now understand that he needed it every bit as much.

EIGHT

The 7 Habits of Equality That Will Change the World

You never change things by fighting the existing reality.
To change something, build a new model that makes
the existing model obsolete.

—Buckminster Fuller

The Fifteenth Amendment to the U.S. Constitution was passed in 1870 giving black men the right to vote. It would take another fifty years for the Nineteenth Amendment to pass in 1920, giving women the same right nationally. Fifty years later, legislation was still needed to outlaw discriminatory practices put in place by southern states to reduce African American eligibility at the polls.

It has been a long road, one we are still traversing, to fully embrace equal rights for all people. It must be stated, again and again, that the only constitutional right guaranteed women in the United States, right now, is the right to vote.

The U.S. Constitution was written by men, for men, at a time when women had virtually no rights. Today most Americans mistakenly believe the U.S. Constitution guarantees equal rights to all people. Many like to cite the Fourteenth Amendment and the Equal Protection Clause (enacted in 1868 on behalf of male slaves) when arguing against the need for the Equal Rights Amendment (ERA). Remember, after the Fourteenth Amendment, women were still not allowed to vote, and thus the need for the Nineteenth Amendment. And while the Fourteenth Amendment has been interpreted in more recent years to protect against discrimination on account of sex, it has not been applied consistently to gender discrimination cases. The ERA will leave no room for doubt that in the United States discrimination on account of sex is prohibited.

As Justice Antonin Scalia said in 2011, it does not:

"Certainly the Constitution does not require discrimination on the basis of sex. The only question is whether it prohibits it. It doesn't."[1]

In 1923, Alice Paul introduced the Equal Rights Amendment, guaranteeing equal rights for all Americans regardless of sex. She well understood that women were not protected from discrimination on account of gender.

The ERA continued to be introduced into every legislative session and finally, in 1972, Congress approved it and did so overwhelmingly: 354–24 in the House and 84–8 in the Senate. It was then sent to the states for ratification—thirty-eight states are required to pass an amendment.

Nevada in 2017, Illinois in 2018, and Virginia in 2020, became the 36th, 37th, and 38th states, respectively, to ratify the Equal Rights Amendment making it our 28th Amendment. It is just twenty-four words:

Equality of rights under the law shall not be denied or abridged by the United States or by any state on account of sex.

So, what is holding it up? There always seems to be something.

In the early 1900s, the argument against the ERA was women's physical stamina and fear that work hours would become too much for the female constitution. In the 1970s, the argument morphed into bathroom usage, the demise of the American family, and fear of women being drafted into the military if equal rights were granted to women. And now, it's an arbitrary deadline that Congress extended once and can be extended again, or simply eliminated.

It is important to remember the Twenty-seventh Amendment, addressing Congressional pay, took more than two hundred years to pass. You know that expression, "the goalpost keeps moving." Well, this one has been moving for a century.

The ERA will undoubtedly be decided by federal courts given the 1982 deadline. Most amendments do not have deadlines. Others have been passed well beyond their deadlines. Some have passed when states that originally approved the amendment rescinded their approval before the amendment reached the thirty-eight-state threshold needed for passage. Hopefully, this will be decided soon and we can say that in the United States of America, our constitution protects the rights of all people, of all genders, and that discrimination on account of sex is prohibited.

In 1973, the Supreme Court decided the case of *Roe v. Wade*, which affirmed a woman's legal right to have an abortion under the Fourteenth Amendment of the Constitution. Although, 77 percent of Americans want *Roe v. Wade* upheld, here we are once again, almost fifty years after its 1973 decision, and we have several states that have passed bills that greatly limit a woman's right to choose what is best for her and her family, getting as close as you can to banning that right altogether.

Although legislation is vitally important, we must continue to seek change at the individual level so that not only do we have laws in place that protect all people from discrimination, we also must become the people who will not abandon them. The pursuit of equality is vital to our very existence. Equality moves societies to their best place because individuals achieve the freedom needed to unleash their full potential.

The first step toward changing the world is to change
our vision of the world and of our place in it.
—Arianna Huffington

I envision a world where people travel freely from one country to another, where cultures are cherished, as are all nationalities, races, ethnicities, religions, sexual orientations, and genders. I see people living peaceful lives, working together to ensure no child dies of starvation or goes uneducated. Our planet is cared for, as we care for our homes and families because we understand at the depths of our souls that the planet is home and we are all family.

Then I envision the kind of people who can make that a reality.

Women, when you value and respect yourself fully, equally, and completely, your work, your history, mind, and heart, the best of humanity will be honored and sought after in every aspect of life.

Men, when you value your whole person, including your loving and nurturing self, you will be strong and fulfilled. You will care for the world in a whole new way, one we are waiting for.

Great people and organizations are working every day to create greater equality in the world. We can all help!

Together we can speed up progress and significantly reduce the estimated hundred years the Global Gender Gap Report tells us we have yet to go before the gender gap is closed.[2] With all hands on deck, or even with most hands on deck, we can accomplish this as we increase awareness, intention, and clarity at the individual level.

We create equality (or lack thereof) through our language, our choices, the traditions we live and pass along, and the beliefs that guide our daily lives. We must become what we seek, prioritizing equality, mindfully living equality, and speaking equality while elevating others to do the same. The payoff for every child, every citizen, every living organism on the planet, and the planet itself, will far exceed the efforts that any one person will ever need to make.

After all, this is mostly about a shift in heart and mind.

I spent a significant portion of my corporate career in the field of market research. Although this is arguably a different arena from social and political research, the underlying social science tenets are largely similar. One of the many wonderful people I was fortunate to work with, while in research, was Eileen Campbell, former CEO, CMO, and board director of several major global companies in the market research and movie industry.

In my research for the book, along with the Global Gender Gap Report, I discovered three additional global reports that add to the story and help guide us. After sharing the data with Campbell, I was excited to hear her say she also felt the data was compelling in light of my book's objective. She suggested I add one more report, the Legatum Prosperity Index™, which I did.

Putting the findings from these five reports, side by side, gives us an exciting vision of where we are heading, all that is at stake, and all that is possible as we work together to close the gender gap once and for all.

The following two tables show the best-performing countries, I call the *Top 20* (Table A), and the worst-performing countries, I call the *Bottom 20* (Table B), from each of the five reports:

▸ Global Peace Index[3]

▸ Global Gender Gap Report[4]

- ▸ World Happiness Report[5]

- ▸ Environmental Performance Index[6]

- ▸ Legatum Prosperity Index™[7]

Then I added two additional pieces of data: the countries that have or have had a woman head of state (these countries are shaded) and the ten most dangerous countries to be female (these countries are capitalized and in bold letters).

THE TOP 20 (TABLE A)

Rank	2018 Global Peace Index	2018 Global Gender Gap Report	2019 World Happiness Report	2018 Environmental Performance Index	2019 Legatum Prosperity Index™
1	Iceland	Iceland	Finland	Switzerland	Denmark
2	New Zealand	Norway	Denmark	France	Norway
3	Austria	Sweden	Norway	Denmark	Switzerland
4	Portugal	Finland	Iceland	Malta	Sweden
5	Denmark	Nicaragua	Netherlands	Sweden	Finland
6	Canada	Rwanda	Switzerland	United Kingdom	Netherlands
7	Czech Republic	New Zealand	Sweden	Luxembourg	New Zealand
8	Singapore	Philippines	New Zealand	Austria	Germany
9	Japan	Ireland	Canada	Ireland	Luxembourg
10	Ireland	Namibia	Austria	Finland	Iceland
11	Slovenia	Slovenia	Australia	Iceland	United Kingdom
12	Switzerland	France	Costa Rica	Spain	Ireland
13	Australia	Denmark	Israel	Germany	Austria
14	Sweden	Germany	Luxembourg	Norway	Canada
15	Finland	United Kingdom	United Kingdom	Belgium	Hong Kong
16	Norway	Canada	Ireland	Italy	Singapore
17	Germany	Latvia	Germany	New Zealand	Australia
18	Hungary	Bulgaria	Belgium	Netherlands	**UNITED STATES**
19	Bhutan	South Africa	**UNITED STATES**	Israel	Japan
20	Mauritius	Switzerland	Czech Republic	Japan	Malta
United States	121	51	19	27	18

Shading represents countries that have/had a woman head of state.
Countries in bold capital letters are most dangerous to be a woman.

THE BOTTOM 20 (TABLE B)

2018 Global Peace Index	2018 Global Gender Gap Report	2019 World Happiness Report	2018 Environmental Performance Index	2019 Legatum Prosperity Index™
Mali	Turkey	Egypt	Cameroon	Libya
Columbia	Cote d'Ivoire	Zambia	Swaziland	**NIGERIA**
Israel	Bahrain	Togo	Djibouti	Mali
Lebanon	**NIGERIA**	**INDIA**	Papua New Guinea	Ethiopia
NIGERIA	Togo	Liberia	Eritrea	Niger
Turkey	Egypt	Comoros	Mauritania	Cameroon
North Korea	Mauritania	Madagascar	Benin	Haiti
PAKISTAN	Morocco	Lesotho	**AFGHANISTAN**	Congo
Ukraine	Jordan	Burundi	**PAKISTAN**	Mauritania
Sudan	Oman	Zimbabwe	Angola	Angola
Russia	Lebanon	Haiti	Central African Republic	**SYRIAN ARAB REPUBLIC**
Central African Republic	**SAUDI ARABIA**	Botswana	Niger	Sudan
DEM REP CONGO	Iran, Islamic Rep	**SYRIA**	Lesotho	Burundi
Libya	Mali	Malawi	Haiti	Eritrea
YEMEN	**DEM REP CONGO**	**YEMEN**	Madagascar	**SOMALIA**
SOMALIA	Chad	Rwanda	Nepal	**DEM REP CONGO**
Iraq	**SYRIA**	Tanzania	**INDIA**	**AFGHANISTAN**
South Sudan	Iraq	**AFGHANISTAN**	**DEM REP CONGO**	Chad
AFGHANISTAN	**PAKISTAN**	Central African Republic	Bangladesh	Central African Republic
SYRIA	**YEMEN**	South Sudan	Burundi	**YEMEN**

Shading represents countries that have/had a woman head of state. Countries in bold capital letters are most dangerous to be a woman.

Campbell's vast experience spanning decades in the research industry analyzing, summarizing, and presenting key findings from complex research studies was too hard to pass up. So, when she sent me her assessment of the data from Tables A and B, I asked her if I might include her conclusions in the book in her words. Not only a brilliant researcher, she is also one of the most generous people I have had the honor to work alongside. Campbell graciously accepted, although she did say crediting her was not necessary. She's also humble.

In Campbell's words:

Regardless of how you may personally define success, it is likely covered in at least one of these reports. While we know that correlation does not equal causality, the results are unmistakably and clearly correlated. On every single metric Levin looked at, the leading countries were much more likely to have been led by a woman, either currently or at some point in modern history. Equally remarkable, the countries that lagged on these important metrics were much less likely to have ever had a female leader. On every single metric—peace, gender equity, the environment, happiness, and economic prosperity—the relationship was consistent. As exhibited in the following table, you will see that countries accepting (or perhaps even embracing) women in roles of political leadership fare remarkably better.

Countries that have/ had women heads of state	Global Peace Index	Global Gender Gap	World Happiness	Environmental Performance Index	Prosperity Index
% of Top 20	75%	85%	70%	65%	75%
% of Bottom 20	30%	15%	35%	35%	20%

While women remain woefully underrepresented in boardrooms and C-suites around the world, there is a growing body of quantitative evidence that indicates when they are present, companies are likely to be more successful.[8] As the body of evidence builds for the power of gender diversity in business, we also have ample evidence that female leadership might also have a similar positive effect on countries.

Lynn Taliento and Anu Madgavkar of the McKinsey Global Institute found evidence that women in positions of political power have different priorities and make different choices in office. They cite one cross-country study that indicates that higher female representation in parliaments led to higher expenditures on education as well as to reductions in corruption. Their research also has shown that nonprofits with women in leadership roles are more successful than those without women in leadership roles in terms of accomplishing both their mission and goals.[9]

Other key findings from Tables A and B show a clear connection between equality, peace, happiness, a healthier environment, and prosperity:

The best countries at closing the gender gap are the most peaceful.
- ▸ Eleven of the Top 20 countries in the Global Gender Gap Report also rank in the Top 20 countries in the Global Peace Index—ten of the eleven have/had a woman head of state.

The best countries at closing the gender gap are the most prosperous.
- ▸ Eleven of the Top 20 countries in the Global Gender Gap Report also rank in the Top 20 countries in the Legatum Prosperity Index—ten of the eleven have/had a woman head of state.

The most peaceful countries are the happiest.

▸ Thirteen of the Top 20 countries in the Global Peace Index also rank in the Top 20 in the World Happiness Report—eleven of the thirteen have/had a woman head of state.

The most peaceful countries are best on the environment.

▸ Eleven of the Top 20 countries in the Global Peace Index also rank in the Top 20 in the Environmental Index—nine of the eleven have/had a woman head of state.

The most prosperous countries are the most peaceful.

▸ Fourteen of the Top 20 countries in the Legatum Prosperity Index also rank in the Top 20 in the Global Peace Index—twelve of the fourteen have/had a woman head of state.

The most prosperous countries are best on the environment.

▸ Fifteen of the Top 20 countries in the Legatum Prosperity Index also rank in the Top 20 countries in the Environmental Performance Index—eleven of the fifteen have/had a woman head of state.

Campbell added:

A remarkable group of countries can be found in the Top 20 on every one of the lists analyzed. This 'champions league' of nations includes Denmark, Finland, Germany, Iceland, Ireland, New Zealand, Norway, Sweden, and Switzerland. Of these, all but Sweden has or had a female head of state. It is noteworthy that the country often perceived as the world's most powerful, the United States, only makes the Top 20 on two of the lists analyzed, weighing in at eighteenth in the Prosperity Index and nineteenth in the Happiness Report. Needless to say, the United States has not elected a female president, and the 2020 election once again shows the resistance to female leadership, particularly at the top.

As I neared the end of analyzing the data from these five reports, I thought it would also be interesting to see where the ten most dangerous countries in the world to be a woman fell within the rankings. According to the *Thomson Reuters Foundation Annual Poll*, the United States had been added to the top ten list in their most recent survey (2018) and is now considered to be the tenth most dangerous country in the world to be a woman.[10]

It is interesting to see that *all* of the other nine countries on the top ten list of most dangerous countries to be a woman can be found in the Bottom 20 (Table B) and in fact congregate toward the lower half of the list (the worst of the worst-performing countries across the five reports).

The top ten most dangerous countries in the world to be a woman include the following:

**India (#1) Afghanistan (#2) Syria (#3) Somalia (#4)
Saudi Arabia (#5) Pakistan (#6) Democratic Republic of Congo (#7)
Yemen (#8) Nigeria (#9) United States (#10)**

Just two of these ten countries (India and Pakistan) have/had a woman head of state.

Campbell concluded her findings by saying, "We can debate correlation versus causation endlessly. Do female leaders drive progress or are progressive countries more likely to elect women? To which I answer, 'Who cares?' The end result of inclusive political leadership appears irrefutable."

Quality of life—peace, happiness, the environment, prosperity, and safety—are tied to how women are represented, included, and treated within a nation and world. After all, women are half a nation's population and potential.

It is not the presence of men that holds us back—it is the absence of women, the absence of diversity. Diversity brings greater balance and wholeness to the leadership team, broader issues to the table, and optimized and creative solutions that are best for all.

It is time to pay great attention to the results women bring to leadership positions whether it's at the peace table, in the halls of Congress and Parliament, or in the boardroom. It is time to focus our attention on the gender gap and all that comes to a nation and the world as the gap closes, as we restore balance within the individual, the organization, and government. And as we close the gender gap, I will assert, we also become the electorate that will put those in office who understand that their power, granted by the people, is for the people—all people. All this has to happen at the most local level there is—you.

Which Brings Us to the 7 Habits of Equality.

You might be wondering how I selected seven when there are so many gender-based norms, beliefs, and traditions steeped in double standards and inequalities. It's a good question.

With a little more than six decades behind me now, these are not only the things that irk me the most, but they have brought on some of the greatest resistance from people when I speak about them. I've learned over time, that where there is resistance, where there is discomfort, oftentimes just beyond that lies our greatest opportunity for growth, improvement, and in this case, equality.

I'm reminded of the person who goes to see their doctor with chest pains. When the doctor informs the patient they have heart disease, the worst news for the patient is not the poor health of their heart. It is the doctor's suggestion to eat more vegetables.

Once you take on a new habit, in this case eating more vegetables, greater well-being is achieved, which not only benefits you but also your family as well. As a matter of fact, we all do, because as sick-care costs come down, so do insurance premiums. As sick days are reduced, there is less strain on the family, on the team at work, and on and on.

I used to play a board game called *Life* for hours at a time with my sisters and brother when we were kids. Moving from college, career, family, and retirement, you move your pawn along the winding path of life. I remember the little $100,000 bills you might be so fortunate to collect along the way.

Think of a similar game board, moving your pawn along the winding path of your life, advancing as you take on a new habit. On this game board, you are not collecting money along the way that leaves some with and some without. This game board provides equality, and peace, and all the benefits that come with it, such as well-fed and educated children, careers, abundance, safe homes, and a peaceful and healthy planet as you move your pawn away from your starting position. As many of my ancestors would ask (albeit most likely about food or their grandchildren), "What's not to love?"

Our current state and starting position on the game board represents the status quo, where we are now with all the choices we have made and traditions we've passed along, to date, individually and collectively. Many of them have resulted in grim statistics and struggles.

At our starting position, there is fear, imbalance, scarcity, and corrupt power that shapes our lives and the world we live in. As each of us moves away from this starting position, the status quo, and toward the top of the game board, we all move. We move toward greater abundance, prosperity, whole and balanced people caring for one another, securing a brighter day and future.

To move up the winding road, away from the status quo, you are simply choosing Habits of Equality. In time, they become our norms, traditions, and beliefs. Remember John Dryden's quote, "We first make our habits and then our habits make us." As you approach the finish line with each new habit of equality instilled in your life, we approach the prize.

As is true when we choose habits of health, unplugging from habits of disease, we begin to feel less discomfort and better health. As we live more Habits of Equality, we see the news getting better, more hopeful, and inspiring. People are happier, uplifted by the good news of the day and the improving quality of their lives—equal pay, equal health care, equal representation, and opportunities. Violence and fighting in the world are letting up, kids are graduating high school well prepared for higher education and/or jobs with living wages. We see pollutants coming down and our planet healing.

There's one more thing before you begin your journey and put your pawn on the game board. One or more of the 7 Habits of Equality might not seem important to you. They might not be news to you. They might not seem relevant to you.

I simply ask that you push ahead and see if there is someplace in your life where you are plugging into inequality or can help someone else unplug. In some way, most of us are either benefiting from inequality, at the expense of others or subordinating ourselves.

No matter how small the impact might seem to you, another choice in alignment with our goal of equality can make a profound difference. The ripple effect from new choices, the way you speak and the things you speak up for, the changes you make in your life, and the model you become for others, create the words of history books to come. These same choices decide the heads of states to be elected, the laws enacted, the judges on the bench, the movies to be written, the children to be saved, and a planet to be healed.

No matter what part you play, I simply ask that you play. Just by getting off of *start*, we all win.

Much like the beautiful butterfly flapping its wings in China shifting the weather in Poughkeepsie, New York, a baby girl, born in sub-Sahara will be well fed and educated, pursuing her own business because she won't be forced into marriage at fourteen years of age as were her mother and grandmother. And this young woman's healthy children and thriving community will live in peace and abundance because you connected another dot in your life to equality. Like the butterfly, we each have the potential to make a profound impact in the world.

Moment by moment, by way of our choices, each of us can help speed up progress in closing the gender gap and finish this unfinished business of our time. Let's rewire the neural circuitry of our own brains by making different choices so that together we can rewire our constitutions, laws, norms, daily practices, and traditions. It is our responsibility to make equality and peace a top priority, and it is our time to do so.

The 7 Habits of Equality that will change the world . . .

Start the Kids Off Equally with One Identity—A Human Identity

Let's teach both girls and boys that the quality of their lives depends on the quality of their relationships, to self and to others, human and nonhuman animals, and our ecosystem. Everyone, regardless of gender identity or expression, needs care and love and the ability to express and process their emotions to thrive and realize their full potential.

A single human identity based on love, compassion, and connection, and the ability to feel and express one's emotions, are essential for a successful and fulfilling life.

Since 2003, I have been a HeartMath® Certified Coach. HeartMath is one of the best approaches out there, with science-based techniques and technology, that destress the body on demand and rewire neural circuitry.[11] Our responses to life, regardless of how difficult an event or circumstance might be, shift to positive responses, well thought out and considered, as we use the HeartMath techniques.

Fear-based feelings like anxiety, anger, frustration, depression, and overwhelm are replaced with love, compassion, and appreciation, thereby creating new neural pathways for future responses that are positive and best for all concerned. We become far less anxious and far more resilient, able to respond to life's events positively and peacefully.

Gender-based identities create response patterns to life that have been reinforced over and over again by society, females acting one way, males another. Because females are generally raised and socialized to be more connected to their hearts, and to their feelings, and to prioritize relationships, we have come to believe it is biology. It is not. That's another story we have told ourselves again and again.

All human beings have the capacity to feel and express their emotions in a healthy manner when they are raised to do so. I have coached hundreds of people over many years to learn the HeartMath techniques to reconnect to their hearts and live their lives from the heart instead of from fear and limitations. When attitudes and neural patterns shift from limited and restrictive gender identities to attitudes and patterns originating from love and appreciation, we are free to live our greatest potential rather than our greatest fears—true for all people, all genders.

It's time to let the binary, gender-based identities go and replace them with a human identity, first and foremost. We are at our best when we are caring and cared for, and there is nothing weak about either. We are most connected when we can share our feelings. There is nothing weak about being connected. In fact, it makes us stronger. We are most fulfilled when we are living to our fullest potential, expressing our opinions, and sharing our talents and skills with the world.

So any colors for the new baby are good, and the best toys are the ones that create the skill sets and neural patterns for self and social awareness, creativity, curiosity, and respect for life in all its diversity. From a shared human identity, love, compassion and kindness, and full expression of our emotions, we can co-create a world that honors each of us equally and fully—one human identity for all.

Start the Marriage/Family on Equal Footing

Here are some ways to move forward in marriage and partnership that will start you off on equal footing.

There's no need to wait for a proposal or an invitation for a date. Although women have been raised and trained to wait to be asked and be acted upon, equality calls you forth and lays the groundwork for an equal partnership in the future. Moving forward requires we act differently than we have done. Go for it, for a life together based on equality from day one—the first date, the engagement, and marriage.

Note to men: feeling uncomfortable with women asking you out or proposing? Notice the discomfort, and think what that's about. The male identity has trained men they are to be in control, to dominate or risk their manhood. Insanity. If we want a true partner in life (or in business or government), it's not going to come with domination and control. This adds undue pressure for men and causes entitlement and privilege at the expense of their well-being and the females of the world. Equality is on the other side of letting go of this fear with greater fulfillment and more peaceful days to come.

I encourage people to have a conversation about names when getting married, a family name, if just one is desired, and children's last name if children are desired. There are so many options, and what is important to hold true is that the family name of one person is as important as the other.

It might help to think of all the countries women keep their names; some even have laws in place prohibiting a name change at marriage such as Greece, France, Italy, the Netherlands, and Belgium. In Malaysia and Korea, women keep their birth names, along with Spanish speaking countries, where children are given both parent's last names. In an effort to create greater gender equality, Quebec passed a law in the mid-1970s prohibiting women from changing their names at marriage to their husbands.[12]

It's always a choice, for either of you, to change your name if you want one family name. Unfortunately in the United States it is pretty much expected that if anyone is going to change their name, it's going to be the woman. Only when we see the same number of men as women changing their last names in marriage, for those who want one family name, that's when we've moved closer to gender equality. Why would full equality include anything short of that?

In our not too distant history, men held all the power, along with the land, the right to be educated, hold a job, control all family finances, and bequeath guardianship of the children to anyone he wanted to upon his death. Like the assumptions that her last name and the children's last name will become his at marriage, these are all habits of inequality.

This one can make people uncomfortable because it goes against a major grain in American society. Please remember the current grain is inequality. That's even more uncomfortable. Look back at those statistics in chapter four.

Women, if you want to walk down the aisle, you can walk yourself down the aisle. Or you can walk *with* whomever you choose—Mom included. Notice the change of language here from the disempowering "walking you home" or "walking you down the aisle" to "walking with you." If both your parents are at the wedding, honor them equally rather than only Dad, who traditionally walks alongside his daughter, while Mom sits on the sidelines.

Let's elevate the women in the wedding party, as we do for men. Men in the wedding party are respectfully called groomsmen and a best man. So brideswomen and best woman will respectfully identify the women in the wedding party as we do the men. There is that squiggly red line again in Microsoft Word under brideswomen but not for groomsmen, letting us know that brideswomen is not a recognized word. Let's change that soon.

Let's make "maids" and "matrons" a memory, and put them where they belong, in the history books, along with the petticoats and corsets. Look up the definition of maids—"a female domestic servant." Now think of the idea that is perpetuated when women are called bridesmaids, whereas men are called groomsmen.

Consider "I now pronounce you wife and husband" versus "man and wife" (that's a major habit of inequality) or "husband and wife"—in most references men go first. Switch it up a bit.

Consider "You may now kiss one another" rather than "you may now kiss the bride," leaving the woman yet again to be acted upon, and "you" being inferred is "the man." We must shift our language so that women are not subsumed by it to have marriages, cultures, and societies that do not do the same.

And of course let's change the infamous statement at the end of the ceremony to something like, "Let me be the first to introduce the married couple, Rhonda and James versus let me be the first to introduce Mr. and Mrs. _____ (usually his last name, which we've covered)."

Connect the dots from marriage, family, to life, and we can create a much better world when we begin the family on equal footing. The children of the world will then expect nothing less than equality from one another and naturally treat others the same way. They will go out into a fair and equal world, living their best life, which you have so beautifully modeled for them.

Call Her a Woman

When gender is relevant, the most respectful thing you can call a woman is a woman, not a girl—just as we call males men when they reach adulthood. Girls are children, as are boys. When we shift away from the gender bias in our language, we elevate women to their rightful place—worthy of the same respect, pay, and opportunities as men.

Using the word "lady" interchangeably with woman sheds more light on why we so often hear people refer to the female boss as a bitch and women running for head of state as harsh, aggressive, and shrill. After all, they are not acting like a lady.

"Lady" implies a type of behavior, as does gentleman; however, the word gentleman, like boy, is not used interchangeably for the men of the world. This is why so many struggle still today seeing a woman too close to the Oval Office, other than a First Lady.

Look at how tough people have been on U.S. First Ladies who have been outspoken, basically anything other than a narrow vision of womankind. Think about the title, First Lady, and the fact that "lady" is part of it, and with it comes an expectation, and a role, usually including guest lists and china patterns.

What a waste of human potential it is when we force people into a role based on their ascribed gender at birth, to live out a gender-based role, when so much more can come from a person's life. This is perhaps a good time to remember the countries that have elected women heads of state and all the advantages these countries have—greater peace, prosperity, happiness, and cleaner and healthier environments.

Instead of Mrs. or Miss, let's use Ms. as men use Mr. their whole lives, or Mx., or nothing at all other than one's name.

This is another important way to end a double standard. Sharing one's marital status is not relevant for a woman when she signs her name, as it is not relevant for a man. This is another relic of history when marital status defined a woman's place in society. It's time for it to go.

Respect and Appreciate Kind, Caring, and Peaceful Men

Who doesn't want a kind, caring, and peaceful father? Who doesn't want a kind, caring, and peaceful friend, spouse/partner, boss, elected official? It is as essential for a peaceful and happy family as it is workplace and nation.

Not only do we need to raise boys with the end game in mind, but also it must be front and center throughout our lives. We must appreciate and respect men who give up that old (so old) macho male identity of power over people, domination of women, and winning at all costs with success too often defined by a bank account, make and model of a car, sex, and greed.

We have a much better chance of survival when we turn the corner on this one. In our homes, on the street, and among world leaders, we need people who are empathic and caring. It's time to heal and become the amazing beings we are. Our greatest strength as human beings, and best opportunity to sustain ourselves and live peacefully, is our ability to love and care for one another as equal and caring partners for life.

Speak Equality

What we call ourselves and others creates energy that is either negative or positive, neural patterns that are either healthy or unhealthy, and opportunities and living conditions that are either good or bad.

Sexist language and name-calling fall into all negative categories, negative energy, unhealthy neural patterns, and unequal opportunities and living conditions. When we speak equality we lift everyone up because we are all affected by the well-being of girls and women.

Pay attention when you hear phrases like "man of the house" and "she doesn't work," and challenge them. Men, when you hear other men calling men ladies as an insult, call them on it. When you hear your friends, family members, and colleagues speak disparagingly about females, intervene.

Speak up for equality. Please don't miss an opportunity to make a positive difference. Remaining silent is a habit of inequality and fuels the epidemic rates of violence against girls and women.

And Mr. Mom? He's not Mr. Mom because it is as much his role to be a dad, including housework, as it is hers to be a mom.

What goes around comes around, and when equality goes around, it comes around in the form of greater safety, acceptance, opportunity, support, and care. Connect the dots from your language to equality, and we'll get there sooner, word by word.

Vote Equality

Constitutional Equality

The majority of Americans believe women are guaranteed equality in the U.S. Constitution. Let's make it clear that nowhere in the U.S. Constitution is discrimination based on sex prohibited.

The Equal Rights Amendment (ERA) will finally put the protection of women's rights in the U.S. Constitution. We're so close. It's our responsibility and our time to make it happen.

Equal Representation

In government, business, schools, and universities, let's make equal representation a goal—equal representation in the movies, in history books, on the front pages of newspapers, including business and sports sections, and nothing less. Look around the table. If all you see are people that look like you, speak up, challenge it, bring in diversity, and reap the benefits.

Talk to the teachers at your children's schools about the history books they are using. Do they equally include the contributions of women? Do your local newspapers cover girls' and boys' sports equally? What we are recording today will land in the history books to come. It's up to each of us to make sure the whole story is recorded.

Equal Pay

For those managing people on the job, you've got a big opportunity to right a terrible wrong—earning 20 percent less than men and even less for women of color, Hispanic, and Native American women. It leaves so many women and children impoverished and women struggling in their later years.

Go on Glassdoor.com and other websites that share company reviews by employees, salaries, and bonuses by position. If you are receiving less pay and you believe it is due to gender, speak up sooner than later so that twenty years down the road, you haven't left hundreds of thousands of dollars in the corporate coffers when the money was rightfully yours.

Freedom to Make One's Own Health Care Choices

As men have total say over their health care choices, so must women. What laws are there that regulate the male body? What political discussions are there about men's health care choices? What conversations are we having about men's behavior as it relates to contraception, pregnancy, vasectomies, and child care? I believe the answer to these questions is none, none, and not enough. If these are personal, private conversations between doctors and men, they must be for women as well.

Equal Work at Home

We will achieve equality outside the home only when we have it inside the home. The United States is the only country of forty-one countries, reviewed by the Organization for Economic Cooperation and Development (OECD), to have no national parental paid leave program as of 2018.

Estonia has eighty-six weeks of paid parental leave, followed by Bulgaria, Hungary, Japan, Lithuania, Austria, Slovakia, Latvia, Norway, and Slovenia—all with at least one year paid parental leave. Two months is the least offered by forty of the forty-one countries on the list. Again, only the United States offers no national parental leave plan. The states of California, New Jersey, Rhode Island, New York, District of Columbia, and Washington have state-mandated paid leave plans in place today.

Of the forty-one countries in the OECD data, thirty-four have money specifically designated for fathers. Japan designates half of paid leave for fathers, and Korea designates fifteen weeks to fathers. Portugal, Norway, Luxembourg, Sweden, and Iceland designate at least two months for new fathers.

I think it is generally accepted that it is important to do our fair share, and that can't stop at the front door. When two adults are present in the household, and both work outside the home, it is vitally important to divide the work at home equitably, including child care. Generally speaking, women carry much more of the workload at home, between housework and the care of children, making it difficult to be at the top of their game, either at home or at work away from home. The impact on their long-term financial well-being is oftentimes disastrous.

Everyone benefits when equality is present in the home, and children, by way of the equal example set for them, will keep it going. It must start there.

Age with Grace

If you are fortunate enough to have grandparents in your life, reach out to them often. The stories, wisdom, and life lessons they share will be time well spent.

After my mother passed away, and throughout my teen years, some of my favorite times were sitting with my grandmothers listening to the stories of their lives. I learned time is precious, and appreciating the years is a more healthy and peaceful way to live.

As a matter of fact, in the healthiest cultures in the world, the elderly are revered. They age more healthily knowing they will always be respected and cared for. Their stories matter, as do their opinions. They live among their loved ones and in communities that care for and support one another throughout a lifetime. Often they work until the end of their lives. Physically they have fewer health issues, and far less heart disease, type 2 diabetes, depression, dementia, and obesity. Many are climbing hills and taking care of gardens and vineyards until their final days.

What they are not doing is spending hours every month and umpteen dollars coloring their hair, having surgeries to alter their bodies to be something they never will be again. There is great freedom in embracing the changes and stages we go through as human beings. We give our children the gift of aging gracefully as they see their loved ones age with grace and ease.

Our habits make us who we are, individually and as a society. To see change, we must *be* the change. The more we are living free of gender biases, the sooner we get to the top of the game board and capture the prize—peaceful people, peaceful homes and communities, a well-cared-for and peaceful world.

It begins with a human identity. It is reinforced by a society that prioritizes equality so that everyone has a fair shot. To reach the state of equality we must choose it with our words, our choices, our traditions, and our votes.

Whether it be more vegetables on the plate or more women at the peace tables around the world, we all win. We become our habits. Let's choose healthy and equal ones.

NINE

Voices of the Future

I may not have gone where I intended to go,
but I think I have ended up where I need to be.

—Douglas Adams

It's been a rather bumpy road these last six decades. Although that void in my heart has never completely filled since the early loss of my mother, it paved the way to observe life in a unique way. Of course, I would have loved more years with her as well as college years and young adulthood free of sexual harassment and assaults. But I had a different lens on the world as a result, which has always served to inspire me to learn more, take risks, and speak out.

I was able to see the importance of having access to all human emotions, no matter how we define our gender. This is vital to living a fulfilling and peaceful life, to having a sense of wholeness and competency in our relationships, and in the pursuit of happiness and success.

I've learned that the more I blamed and shamed, the less I was available to care and share. Time is precious, so I have become a better steward of it. Instead of using time and energy on what happened last month or forty years ago, more often than not, I choose to use my energy and time to secure what I do want—a safe and just world, greater happiness, and health.

I've learned that as we dig in and point fingers, we keep the status quo in place. After all, we're stuck ourselves. We can all find plenty of evidence of wrongdoing, privilege, prejudice, and injustice out there in the world as well as within ourselves. There is also plenty of evidence of right-doing, of positive change, and of those choosing a new course that will ultimately change the status quo and history.

I love to think about those historic two days in 1848 when three hundred women and men came together to attend a women's rights convention in Seneca Falls, New York. This was the first time a convention for women's rights had taken place in the United States.

Abolitionists and women's rights activists Lucretia Mott and Elizabeth Cady Stanton were the key organizers. The two women had met in London in 1840 for the World Anti-Slavery Convention. When they arrived, they were denied seating with the men and taken to a designated area for women. They returned to the United States knowing they must work for women's rights as well.

The final document emerging from the Seneca Falls Convention was called the Declaration of Sentiments. Despite opposition, the leaders moved ahead and included a woman's right to vote in the final document. It would take another seventy-two years before the Nineteenth Amendment would pass, granting American women voting rights. Few of those who fought so long and hard for the right to vote would live to cast their own.

From three hundred attendees in Seneca Falls, the number swelled to 17,000 to 22,000, heading to Houston, Texas, for the 1977 National

Women's Conference. The conference brought leaders from all over the country, including politicians, journalists, photographers, and several First Ladies, both Democrat and Republican. All major news stations were there. According to Dorothy Spruill's book, *Divided We Stand: The Battle Over Women's Rights and Family Values That Polarized American Politics*, "When Egyptian president Anwar Sadat suddenly decided to make his historic journey to Israel, they had to send their B teams: the A teams were already in Houston."[1]

Living in St. Louis at the time, I remember the excitement around the conference and the high hopes that it would help us pass the ERA. Unfortunately across the Mississippi River came the opposition, led by Phyllis Schlafly.

My friends and I couldn't reconcile Schlafly's strong opposition to women taking on any other role than homemaker when she herself was a Washington University law school graduate, a candidate for Congress on multiple occasions, and one of the most ardent leaders of the conservative, antiwomen's rights movement. Schlafly's own mother entered the workforce to keep the family afloat and her daughter in private school because Schlafly's father was unemployed for long periods of time.

"Women have two choices," according to Gloria Steinem. "Either she's a feminist or a masochist." There will always be those opposing change, those who stand for the status quo of their time. There is much they have invested in, long-standing traditions, a way of life and livelihood, and the power to keep things as they are. What they do not realize is that their lives and their children's lives improve as the community and the nation grow stronger, when each of us has equal opportunities and freedom to live our full potential. Anything less than that creates conflict in a country and in the world.

Imagine the joy Elizabeth Cady Stanton and Lucretia Mott would have felt had they been with us on January 21, 2017, for the Women's March in Washington, D.C., the largest, single-day protest in U.S.

history on behalf of women's rights. What began as a U.S. march in cities around the country became a worldwide demonstration of millions to support human rights, immigration reform, religious freedom, health care and reproductive rights, workers' rights, and protection of the environment. Three to 5 million Americans and 7 million people around the world participated.

I attended the 2017 Women's March in Washington, D.C., as did my family and friends. It was a proud moment for me, a feminist virtually my entire life. Like so many, I felt robbed of our first woman U.S. president in 2016 due largely to misogyny, corruption, and greed. It was life-affirming to be among so many people, coming together on one single day, peacefully, joyfully, and with a commitment to all of humanity and to the planet. *That's how powerful and peaceful we can be.*

No matter the bumps in the road, I like to remember those three hundred women and men in Seneca Falls at a time when women had virtually no rights. They lit the way for us to keep moving along this bumpy path, one generation after another. What seemed radical to think about during the mid-1800s are the norms of our time.

Bumps and all, you can't stop progress born from the most powerful energy of all. Love trumps fear and hate every time. Loving human beings, respecting and supporting all other human beings, their rights, their desires, and potential, that is what will resolve our greatest challenges.

So where are we heading? I reached out to younger generations to find out. I'm happy to say that, it looks as if we're going to be in great hands.

Michelle, forty-two, married and adopting

I was excited to speak with Michelle about her experience in the United States now that gay marriage is legal nationwide, hoping to hear even more good news.

Michelle is originally from Colorado and was a teacher in the early years of her career. She described this time as having to wear many hats to keep her sexual orientation private. Michelle came out when she was married in 2015, greatly surprising colleagues she had worked with for years.

"Location, location, location." Michelle told me you have to be careful where you go because it is still dangerous to be gay in certain parts of the country. She said the riskiest places to be are the most religious because of what people are taught in the Bible. "It is considered a sin, and you will go to hell for being gay." Hearing this message much of her life made her feel unworthy, and she became burdened by guilt. "Even the love you feel, you feel guilty about."

Today, Michelle and her wife are excited to become foster parents. On average, Michelle said, foster kids are moved four times a year in the south and LGBTQ+ kids are moved twice as much. That's eight times a year. Michelle feels this is why she is now living in the South, for these kids, who need a family and home they can count on.

After living outside the United States, seeking a place they felt safe to live, foster, and adopt a child, Michelle and her wife are back in the United States. They lived in New Zealand and visited Uruguay for three months because these countries, according to Michelle, are close to perfect when it comes to same-sex couples fostering and adopting children.

Upon coming back to the United States, they learned that five U.S. states had made it legal for same-sex couples to adopt, with equal rights throughout the process. They moved to one of them, North Carolina.

Today, Michelle and her wife are excited about the future, expanding their family, and giving kids a home they can count on. They have started a nonprofit called Angel K Love Project for LGBTQ+ foster children, where kids will find love, support, and security, to be in the world confidently and successfully as they reach adulthood, no matter their location.

Matt, forty-one, married with two young sons

Matt has dedicated his life to the care and well-being of seniors and kids and has a love for music and art. His jobs have usually combined all of the above. He told me he struggles at times to raise his two boys without toxic masculinity. I asked him to tell me more about that.

"For me, it is tied to anger and how I respond to frustration and stress." It's a sense of being right, Matt elaborated, and feeling entitled to call you out, to tell you what is wrong. "And if you don't change your behavior, I'm entitled to change it physically." Although he has not acted upon that inclination, he sees it in other men. "I'm trying not to live that way. I know I'm vulnerable to it."

Matt admitted he doesn't have a great track record. "I was raised with five brothers. My dad is a sweet, sensitive man and pretty masculine as well. I grew up in rural Georgia, filled with toxic masculinity, along with xenophobia, racism, and homophobia. Sports contributes to it a lot there."

"My saving grace is my wonderful mother, who has evolved socially, spiritually, and as a feminist. We are on this journey together. I've also had almost entirely female bosses, and thank goodness for that. That toxic masculinity could have been fueled had I not been."

I asked him how he counteracts these feelings of entitled anger when he disagrees with someone or someone does something he doesn't like. "I'm still trying to figure that out," he told me. "When it occurs I'm quick to realize it. I am quick to apologize and acknowledge any harm I've done. As opposed to holding onto it, I'll take a break and walk away. Then when I come back, I'll apologize."

Because Matt told me he has had mostly female bosses, I was curious if he battles these feelings of entitlement often. In fact, he told me it was the opposite. "Being with women neutralizes it." He shared how much more himself he is, how he feels more balanced, living in line with his true identity when around women. It sounds like a human identity to me.

Matt told me his men friends are the same, all with professional women in their lives working on becoming more aware of male entitlement and toxic masculinity. They come together, Matt said, and talk about how to be great dads and partners.

He shared with me a few more things that have me feeling hopeful about our next generation. When he hears women called girls or bad names, he calls it out. He calls women "women" and girls "girls," as he does for boys and men—boys when they are kids and men when they are adults. He understands women deserve the same respect.

At home, Matt and his wife are focusing on raising their sons differently than they were raised. "If the boys want to paint their fingernails and go to school, that's what they do. When they want to wear pink shoes and wear their hair long, they do," he said. "A color isn't a gender."

When his son went to school one day with his nails polished, another boy asked him why he would do that. Matt's son simply responded, "Because I wanted to," and walked away.

"We want our boys to feel safe and know they can identify themselves however they want and need to, especially because they are adolescents and developing a sense of who they are. They can choose distinct personal pronouns and identify their sexual identity at their own pace. It's okay to be nonbinary. We need to offer more than two boxes for them to check."

Matt wrapped up our conversation by saying he's not perfect and that sometimes his behavior might surprise me. "I'm a work in progress," he humbly stated.

The good news is that perfection is not the goal because perfection is not achievable. Progress is the goal, and progress, when in action, is always within reach.

Tyler, twenty-eight, college student

Tyler, who is twenty-eight and will soon have his college degree, is hopeful about his future. Tyler shared with me he is a biracial trans male, which has undoubtedly given him a deep understanding of ongoing hardships, prejudice, and discrimination. He is most excited about being back in school after several years of taking care of some health issues.

I asked him where he sees gender bias in the United States. "We're socialized by it, so it is a somewhat difficult thing to notice. Girls on the left, boys on the right. Even in school, they are reinforcing gender norms."

This has always been a negative for Tyler and a source of confusion. "Because I'm trans, I'm being pushed to the girls, and I always wanted to go with the boys. Today there is a lot more acceptance. Growing up, I never heard the word transgender."

Tyler said there's still plenty of evidence of gender bias. "Males are allowed to be angry and seen as powerful. Females get angry, and there is something wrong with them. She's out of control. For males it's okay. They're just being authoritative." Whereas Tyler talked about how men aren't allowed to cry, he said he was not limiting himself to a set of emotions. "Gender is what we make it to be."

We talked about male violence against women, and he said that men are taught that it's their right to take, to control and be in charge, which perpetuates rape culture. When it comes to domestic violence, Tyler said, "Abuse is abuse. If you punch someone on the street, you will be arrested, so it shouldn't be okay because it's happening in your home."

We talked a bit about where he sees male entitlement and gender bias in marriage. "There is a lot of sexism and patriarchy in marriage. Rarely does a male take a female's name; it's almost unheard of. It would be like, "'What's wrong with you, man?'" Tyler's solution? "Why not alternate? One child has one parent's name and the other has the other parent's name, and she should get the name of the first child. After all, she did most of the work."

As we were concluding our time together, Tyler gave some great advice, "Change is an uphill battle. The moment we take our foot off the gas, the moment we stop going forward, we start sliding back. Complacency is our worst enemy."

Jaymie, twenty-four years old, political campaign manager for 2020 presidential candidate

Jaymie has been an organizer many of her teen years and at the time of our conversation was part of the lead team for a 2020 presidential candidate. I asked her what she is hopeful about today.

"Young kids in high school who are thinking about politics and gun reform. They are so young and active when they're eighteen. And so many women are not going to help a man to the top. They are going to take themselves to the top."

Jaymie was also excited to be part of a presidential campaign that was being led by so many women of color. As a woman of color herself, she is happy to see others leading the way. She shared a positive insight with me, "Things are going in the right direction even if nationally we don't see it."

She does have concerns, though, such as attacks on women's health care, especially how it affects women in rural areas. Jaymie is from the South, and in the rural communities, they do not have major hospitals. You have to drive an hour or more to find an ob-gyn, and as a result, there are high infant mortality rates. She told me the story of her own health event that almost took her life.

When she was pregnant with her daughter, she felt severe stomach pains one day. Jaymie keeled over in pain and was told to take aspirin. Four hours later she had seizures, and her blood pressure spiked. Her daughter was born at thirty-two weeks, weighing two pounds. If the doctor had taken her more seriously, she feels, the outcome might have been different. She feels fortunate to be here today raising her daughter.

In terms of race, Jaymie said whenever she walks into an interview, her first thought is, "I pray this person is not a racist." With police, she had a troubling response as well, "I pray my body is not a weapon."

Jaymie finds it hard to date men in her community. Because they are men, she said, "I'm supposed to uphold them." The expectation, she said, is that she should be a teacher or a nurse or housewife.

I shared with Jaymie the research that tells us African American women face even more domestic abuse than Caucasian women and are less apt to call the police. Her response was chilling and eye-opening, "If we call the cops, they might shoot him."

This was an important insight, I thought, and reminded me that things can't always be understood by numbers alone. We experience different lives due to our gender and gender identity, sexual orientation, race, religion, our parents, nationality, physical abilities, and so on. Let's keep asking questions.

Allegra, twenty-four, 2019 college graduate

Allegra's mother has been the greatest influence in her life. Her mother was born in Sweden and came to the United States where she earned a PhD from UC Berkeley. She went on to work with women whose lives had been deeply affected by violence. Many were children themselves raising children. Allegra's mother's work and passion for helping these women allowed Allegra to understand how important women's rights are and the inequalities that still remain.

I asked Allegra what sets the United States and Sweden apart as Sweden ranked number 14 in the world in reaching gender equality, whereas the United States ranked number 121 in 2018. She told me about parental leave in Sweden. Mothers and fathers have four hundred days of shared parental leave. Her cousin chose to stay at home and raise the children, while his wife worked outside the home. When the kids were older, he was able to easily reenter the job market with full benefits.

When I asked her what concerned her about gender inequality the most, her voice shifted to a heavier, more serious tone. "I'm concerned about the opportunities I will not have because I am female. The wage gap that many men feel does not exist exists." She went on to say, "Men go into job interviews with overinflated views of themselves, not necessarily based on what they have accomplished, whereas women base their confidence on what they have actually achieved."

Allegra is a two-time sexual assault survivor. After one assault by her boyfriend at the time, she was in shock and traumatized. He apologized for his actions, yet the next day he acted as though nothing had happened. She grew to understand that he acted out of his own anger and insecurities. She said, "Men will take advantage of you if you do not tell them you will not put up with this, and they don't have agency over you." She left that relationship soon thereafter.

We talked a little about marriage and how women are expected to change their names. Allegra said quite firmly, "I would never marry someone who would question me keeping my own name." This passionate young woman, still inspired by her mother and as a recent graduate, is well on her way to making the world a fairer and better place.

Lauren, twenty, graduating class of 2022

Lauren has always wanted to work in the federal government. When she was younger she wanted to be president. Today she wants to be Senate majority leader. She has discovered since the 2016 election, how much power there is in Congress. Being the voice of the people, representing them and their needs, is her dream, and she's going after it.

Right now she is excited about all the different kinds of people she is meeting and learning from. Her mother, she shared with me, has always been that "go-getter kind of woman." Lauren is clearly following in her footsteps.

I asked Lauren what she is most concerned about today. She told me as a bisexual woman, she was concerned about the LGBTQ+ community and felt we have a long way to go in this country to create true gender and sexual orientation equality. Given the little attention to the ruthless killings of trans women of color and others in the LGBTQ+ community, she wants to see greater attention given and representation of the full spectrum of the LGBTQ+ community. "There is more to community besides white cis gay men," she said. "There are nonbinary lesbians, black gay men, disabled gender-fluid queers, and more." Without representation everywhere, from Congress to TV, Lauren said these people struggle to have a strong voice.

She went on to tell me about another pressing concern: climate change. "There will be no people problems if we do not have an earth to have people on, so the environment today is my biggest concern. We have let it go to this point, where we have ten to fifteen years to figure it out."

With regard to gender inequality, she said, "Absolutely it exists. Just yesterday in class they were talking about job qualifications, and gender was part of the discussion, how those hiring view women versus men, and why women are less likely to be hired. If married, her chances are even less because apparently, that means kids and maternity leave. Then there are negotiations. If a woman speaks her mind and says her credentials are outstanding, she is arrogant, demanding, or bossy." In terms of pay, she feels employers are likely to think if you are female then you need to take the job with the pay they are giving you or no job at all.

She shared a personal story of when she was a writer for her school newspaper. Overall, she said it was a positive experience. "I knew what I wanted to write and what I wanted to say. However, many of my ideas were rejected, as were those of other females on staff who had big ideas that could have truly worked. They were too big, too messy, and you have to interview people, at least that was the perception of their editors. Meanwhile, the guys wanted to do another sports story."

She has felt gender bias in her political activities as well. "Being talked down to, interrupted by men in the field—it will take more training for women to say, 'I wasn't finished—that was my idea.'"

She shared her thoughts on how all this has come to be. "Teaching young boys that it's okay to interrupt women. And just because you speak louder, then it's your idea. So it carries on from a very young age."

We talked about race and sexuality. Lauren said, "I know I am a young white woman from a middle-class family. So you can't forget those of color, disabled, transgender, or all three. I know their voices are not even in the conversation. That's not right and needs to change."

Lauren, as is true for the others I spoke with, also has friends who have been sexually assaulted—true for most of us if we were to ask.

In terms of her last name and ever changing it if she were to marry, "I love my last name. It's a powerful name." She said it is totally up to the mother and father. "Change it from one to the other; hyphenate it."

And when it comes to naming children, "He is there for a few minutes, and she carries the child for nine months. It doesn't make a whole lot of sense that the children are always named after him."

"My parents were divorced when I was very young, and my dad would try to show dominance over my mom a lot. Lauren told me one way he would do this was by saying, you're a _____, inserting his last name. I'm not just my dad's child. I'm my mother's child as well."

As I concluded the interview, I asked Lauren what she would like to see women do differently to speed up gender equality. "It's been a long time coming. Hillary Rodham Clinton running for president and now in 2020, so many more women running. Seeing more women represented in politics, in the movies, writers, women of color, gay, fighting for all women, I think that is crucial for us to move on as a gender. More diverse voices in a conversation bring a wealth of possibilities for bigger solutions to come about. We've been trying to come up with a plan in the United States for climate change, and it took a waitress from the Bronx to ask what the hell we are doing. Diversity is vital."

"And what of men? What is their role?" I asked her.

Lauren said it starts in the home. "When they become fathers, when they are making friends, in the workplace, in conversations with men, tell them, instead of talking over women, instead of calling them bossy, why don't we listen to them? Let's see what we can do to make this more equal. Listening is important. Talk to your sons, and say, 'Hey, maybe don't push Sally in the sandbox if you like her; just tell her that and be her friend. Don't catcall women. They are not objects. Women are powerful, helpful, vital people that deserve whatever it is they want to work for. And don't bring it up because you have a sister or a daughter. It doesn't matter that you have women in your life. It should be that women deserve your respect. So listen, have discussions about equality, just because it's the right thing to do."

I see so much wisdom in this young woman, potential, and promise, and I look forward to seeing her in the Senate.

Sydney, nineteen, child of military parents

Sydney spent her childhood moving every four years because both parents are in the military. She will obtain her undergraduate degree in 2022 and hopes to go into politics, either working on her own campaign or in support of a candidate.

She believes her generation will create significant change in the United States. She is, however, concerned about growing white nationalism. She shared with me the moment she realized there was a countermovement to the one she and her peers were a part of, which was all about equality, connection, and shared purpose. She was both surprised and terrified by it.

I asked Sydney how gender inequality has affected her. She replied, "As a woman in leadership roles, no matter how hard I worked and how much I got done, I was always undermined by the dudes behind me talking about my butt. And that goes back to my sophomore year in high school." No matter your reputation or qualifications, Sydney said she was ignored because of her gender. "When men ran the organization, they were allowed to run them. When I ran the same organization, my supervisors didn't allow me to speak or lead." Some women also made it difficult, she pointed out. "They seemed to get offended, like they were telling me, 'You are no better than me.'"

Sydney told me about a situation that came up that morning in class that bothered her. "In language, we were reading the UN's Declaration of Human Rights, and they were changing the pronouns to 'he and him.' It was actually pointed out to us to never say 'hey, gals.' You have to say 'hey, guys.' Well, I would never walk into a room and say 'ladies' in a room of women and men, yet it's okay to do the opposite."

"I don't like being called a girl," Sydney told me, "now that I'm on my own, at college, and not reliant on my parents. If they refer to you as a girl and your male counterpart as a man, that would bother me, and I would say something. I don't like being called a lady either. Language is important. 'Lady' is usually not used in a respectful way. It's suggesting behavior. I need to be a lady, be quiet, be calm, not speak out, act more proper."

Sydney's voice ticked up in excitement when she spoke about the stories of women she was learning about for the first time. During a Civil War project she initiated, she learned about the nurses who were also surrounded by death and turmoil. She said, "Nobody cared about their PTSD or even how skilled they were. We also only spent about a day on the feminist movement but, on Civil Rights, at least a couple of weeks."

One of Sydney's good female friends had been drugged and raped. The rapist kept her at his house for two days. No one knew where she was. When I asked her if her friend pressed charges, Sydney said she did not because she didn't think anyone would care or that it would make a difference. She wanted to forget.

On marriage, Sydney said she will not be changing her name and plans for her children to have her last name. She is proud of her name and Mexican heritage. Sydney had a fight with her boyfriend about this. "I ended it saying, 'I am not giving up my last name for you.' His response was, 'Well, why should I give up my name for you?'" Sydney replied by saying, "Well, that's what you're asking me to do."

"Changing your name and naming your children after him means the male name is more important—everything about him is more important, that his lineage is more important than mine."

We closed our discussion talking about ways we can speed up gender equality. Sydney believed it was in conversations like the one we were having. "Having these conversations is really important because a lot of people don't think about it. Even women I know. They don't care; they don't notice. It's ingrained in them, like the idea that you don't walk alone at night. They don't qualify that as gender inequality. They don't think it's just women that do that."

Sydney wants women to be more open to talking about their experiences because others have gone through something similar. She cited her friend who had been raped and didn't want to tell her. "She was embarrassed. She was afraid to talk about it. I could have been there for her. So be open to talking about things that have happened to you, what you worry about, what you are scared about. Because we have gone through it, too, and don't be afraid to stand up to dudes trying to push you down."

I asked her what can men do. "Be open-minded. Don't assume because I said, 'Hey, that thing you just said or did was sexist,' that I'm calling you a sexist, that I'm attacking you. I'm not. I'm trying to educate you so you don't hurt another woman down the line."

In closing, she shared these powerful words. "No matter what everybody else does, no matter how anyone treats you, make sure you are true to yourself. Push through. Be kind to everyone you know. Don't argue; just inform. That tiny little bit of information you gave them, no matter how badly they took it, can lead them on a completely different path, where they are advocates for you, where they believe in you just as much as you believe in yourself."

That's great advice from a nineteen-year-old!

It's amazing what you learn when you ask questions and listen to the answers. Sharing stories is one of the most powerful ways to deepen our understanding of an issue and one another and move forward with solutions that create positive change that stand the test of time.

I've loved talking to and learning from the generations that follow my own. In spite of the many challenges they are facing, they are hopeful and excited about their futures and all the possibilities the world has to offer them.

The world we can co-create, with equality front and center, living mindfully of the impact of our language, our choices, and traditions, is a peaceful, healthy, and abundant one. Shifting who we hold ourselves to be, in this diverse universe we live in, is the place to start.

Fortunately, more women and men are moving beyond the limitations of predetermined roles in life defined by gender, and instead choosing to follow roles defined by their hearts. Women are following their passions and leading the way inside and outside the home. Men are finding their hearts and actively engaging and caring for their children and, as a result, becoming better corporate and world citizens.

I can barely come up with a reason to check the gender box anymore. I'll say the same thing for the Mr., Miss, Mrs., and Ms. boxes and those asking if I am married, single, or divorced. I write my name on the form and skip a good portion of the things asked, and rarely does anyone say a thing about it. If they do, I ask, "And why do you need to know this?" That usually does it.

Balance and wholeness are restored as we live in sync with what it means to be a human being, not a gendered being pursuing a gender-based definition of success and happiness. Identifying first and foremost as a human being and living in alignment with the health and well-being of self, others, and our planet are ways to restore peace to the world.

So what will speed up equality and peace? Two critical things, as I see it.

1. **Embrace our full humanity as our identity and live the Habits of Equality.**

    We are each loving, caring, and compassionate beings first and foremost. It's how we come into the world and how we are meant to live our lives, caring for ourselves and others.

    Yes, of course, we each have our unique gifts, passions, and goals in life. Let's live them in a way that lifts all of humanity to a higher standard of life, liberty, and happiness with the choices we make on a daily basis.

    What does equality look like day to day? In the morning and evening with family, it's the time for love, caring, and sharing, supporting one another to be our best. It doesn't take ovaries to do that, just a great breakfast, positive emotions, and positive words to start the day. Children need that to thrive, as do adults. That is pure and simple human nature, how we come into the world, and how we can leave it.

    In the day or whenever work comes, we move into action mode. We're creating, leading, producing, coordinating, and collaborating to get a job done. It doesn't take testicles to do that better or at all. And it doesn't mean we leave love, caring, and sharing out of our work—it means we bring it to the job.

The Habits of Equality are both a road map and accelerant to closing the gender gap. It's our habits that create the world we live in and our habits that will change it. Living Habits of Equality is our best way forward and best hope of saving the world and all its precious inhabitants.

2. **Have lots and lots of conversations at home, at work, with friends and family, in the neighborhood, at meetings, at temple, church, the mosque, wherever people come together, to connect, learn, and grow.**

   Share stories, ask lots of questions, listen, and get ready for some of the most rewarding conversations of your life as you learn what it's like to walk in someone else's shoes. Remember, the most creative and effective solutions for our biggest challenges come from a diverse group of minds, along with compassion and empathy.

It's pretty simple, this recipe for equality and peace. The more difficult part for people is letting go of long-standing practices and beliefs steeped in sexism and misogyny, so steeped we call them traditions rather than what they truly are. Just as we wouldn't justify slavery by saying it is tradition or old school, we need that same mindset when it comes to sexism and misogyny. It's not tradition or old school—it's gender apartheid.

Perhaps a helpful reminder is that many of us do not practice religion the same way our parents did or are the first in the family to get a college education. Once we attain that degree or change traditions, we're a changed person, knowing ourselves, and the world, in a whole new way. Awareness, education, and acting in accordance with a mission—that's powerful stuff. Word by word, choice by choice, one action and tradition at a time, we will change the world.

Before you speak you can think about whether the words will denigrate or uplift, will perpetuate a gender-based stereotype or norm, or move us upward on the path to equality. Will the expression, joke, or idea you are about to say help move us closer to closing the gender gap? If not, what about using words of equality instead?

As you make a choice, you can consider whether the choice will perpetuate a gender stereotype and the subordination of others or fuel change. Will it level the playing field, or empower or disempower another human being? As you act, you can ask yourself through the lens of equality, is this going to speed up equality or maintain the status quo?

And as you pass along a tradition within your family, will you take a moment to think about it, consider its origin, and what it continues to reinforce in the family and society. Is it time to create a new tradition, one that is more inclusive, eliminates a double standard, and moves us closer to gender equality?

The most pressing challenges of our time depend upon these moment-by-moment choices we make with our words and actions. When we live our lives with equality as our mission, as we raise our children, go to school and work, be with friends and family, and serve in our communities, each of us has the opportunity to be a piece in the mosaic closing the gender equality gap once and for all.

As we live Habits of Equality we can only create equality, just as we create better health when we live habits of health. It's an organic process, and as we restore health and balance from within, so goes the world.

Poverty

According to the Global Partnership for Education, 171 million people could be lifted out of extreme poverty if all children left school with basic reading skills. "We believe that ensuring quality education for all is not only central to the achievement of all of the Global Goals but in particular the goal to end extreme poverty."[2]

Food and Agriculture Organization of the United Nations (FAO), Director General José Graziano da Silva stated:

Achieving gender equality and empowering women is not only the right thing to do but is a critical ingredient in the fight against extreme poverty, hunger, and malnutrition. Evidence shows that when women have opportunities, the yields on their farms increase—also their incomes. Natural resources are better managed. Nutrition is improved. And livelihoods are more secured.[3]

Closing the gender gap is a game changer in diminishing the rates of poverty, both nationally and globally. One additional year of secondary school for girls increases a family's income by 15–25 percent.[4]

Violence and War

U.N. Women's Executive Director Phumzile Mlambo-Ngcuka tells us when both women and men are at the peace table, agreements "last longer and are more stable."

Writer Soraya Chemaly posits:

What if I suggested that reducing the rates of rape and sexism in the U.S. would reduce our risk of international conflict? You might think that American girls and women who regularly adapt their lives to deal with 'harmless' street harassment, or who are assaulted by American men, have little to do with, say, the Iraq War. Yet research shows an undeniable relationship between the treatment of women in everyday life and a nation's propensity for engaging in war.[5]

The Director of Programs at UN Women, Maria Noel Vaeza, spoke to the "multiple dividends" when gender equality is achieved:

"food security, poverty reduction, better climate management, and peaceful solutions."[6]

Climate Change

A 2018 article from the United Nations connects the gender gap and the health of our planet:

> Successful action on climate change depends on the engagement of women as stakeholders and planners in ensuring that everyone has access to the resources they need to adapt to and mitigate climate change. Climate change cannot be fully addressed by individual countries, but rather requires enhanced global cooperation from both policy-makers and nonparty stakeholders in order to bring women's voices and specific needs to the table.[6]

The International Union for Conservation of Nature (IUCN) shares exciting progress in creating effective and sustainable climate change solutions as women become an integral part of the process:

> Women have proven to be leading the way toward more equitable and sustainable solutions to climate change. Across sectors, women's innovations and expertise have transformed lives and livelihoods, and increased climate resilience and overall well-being. Unleashing the knowledge and capability of women represents an important opportunity to craft effective climate change solutions for the benefit of all.[7]

The countries focusing on the well-being of their citizens understand that their well-being is inextricably linked to the well-being of the environment we live in. As we look to the countries that score highest on the Environmental Performance Index (EPI), we see the same countries that rank at the top of the list for creating equality, peace, happiness, and prosperity.

Science tells us, that time is running out. I believe there are more of us in the world who know this to be true than those who want to maintain the status quo of power, money, and greed at the expense of others and our planet. It doesn't take Stephen Hawking brainpower to understand an unkempt home is not healthy for its inhabitants, nor is an unkempt planet.

The best pathways to reducing poverty and hopelessness, violence, war, and climate change are pathways that provide equal access to opportunities and resources for all people. As we move to a single human identity, with full access to and expression of our emotions, children become more loving, caring, and compassionate adults, concerned for others and the world we live in. Violence, war, and the pursuit of money at the expense of people and planet are no longer viable options, not when your identity and success are defined by your ability to care, love, and help one another.

My heart continues to heal from the early loss of my mother and the pain I felt from violence and inequities throughout my lifetime. As each of us does our part, planting seeds of justice in lieu of seeds of injustice, I know our greatest challenges—violence, war, poverty, and climate change—can finally, and once and for all, be behind us.

What became apparent to me early in life is that it is time for the patriarchy to be dismantled in every country in the world. There is no more important work today than that of equality.

We understand the civil rights of all human beings are inextricably linked. If we are to reduce and eliminate our greatest challenges, ensuring that everyone has a fair shot at life must be our goal.

We are on one team, and it's called humanity. We live in different countries on this beautiful planet, in different communities, and in different families. Yet we are all human beings deeply connected to one another and our planet, desiring love, freedom, safety, and the opportunity to achieve happiness and success.

For peace and a healthy sustainable planet, we need each person to be strong, to be healthy, to be free.

To be equal.

We're on our way. Let's speed it up!

Acknowledgments

No other topic has captured my heart and attention for as long as this one has. I am truly thankful for all of life's experiences. It is in the struggle we come to know peace. I am so grateful for those who have been part of this journey with me, and I thank you from the bottom of my heart.

My mother, Mildred Burgess Levin—although you didn't get to see my twelfth birthday, you made a world of difference to me. You were my champion. Your love of family, learning, and speaking your truth live on. My father, Martin Levin—your transformation to provider of unconditional love and support inspires me to speak with compassion and hope. Never give up, no matter the obstacle, and always, always pay attention to those with less good fortune. This was your way of life and lessons passed on for a life well-lived.

Alenna Levin Schneider, you are the love of my life and the one most of all who has shown me what peace and equality truly look like as you boldly and kindly live your life. And Kev, together you two are the embodiment of loving and equal partnership.

My brother and sisters: Mark Levin, Cindy Levin, and Cathy Levin; and their spouses, Becky Levin, Jeff Schrieber, and Driss Senhaji—you provided the love and support I needed to get through the toughest of times and the laughs that kept me sane. My nieces and nephew: Alex, Samantha, Ranya, and Naim—it is wonderful being in this world with you. Watching you earn degrees and find success and happiness are the best reminders that we are making progress and to keep on keepin' on.

Lynda Goldman, Carol Denker, and Helen Wilkie, thank you for being the brilliant writing professionals you are, challenging me to clarify, stay on task, and get it done.

Thank you to friends and family who read a chapter or more and provided their insights, opinions, writing, and grammar skills with me: family—Mark, Cindy, Cathy, and Alenna, and friends—Melissa Klearman, Robert Brandon, Sandy Hook, Rebecca Now, and Karen Dwyer. And here's another shout-out for Robert for the many hours-long conversations about gender, race, culture, and politics that had me see things in a whole new way.

Thank you, Eileen Campbell, friend, mentor, and market research guru. Eileen volunteered to help me summarize hundreds of data points as only she can do—brilliantly with a deep understanding and passion for equality and fair play.

To Michelle, Matt, Tyler, Jaymie, Allegra, Lauren, and Sydney for your contribution to the final chapter of this book and the next chapter of our lives. Your passion and commitment to a more fair, sustainable, and kinder world give us hope and inspiration.

Lynn Povich, Maxine Clark, Mark Levin, Gloria Feldt, and Zaron Burnett III—thank you for allowing me to share our conversations. Your energy, ideas, and commitment to what can be rather than what is will never stop making a positive difference in the world.

And for all those who have come before us, who have stood up, spoken out, and gone against the grain, we stand on your shoulders and will continue to light the way forward—on our way to equality and peace.

Notes

Introduction

1. Ijeoma Oluo, *So You Want to Talk About Race*, copyright © 2019, reprinted by permission of Seal Press, an imprint of Hachette Book Group, Inc., 74–75.

2. From THE MOMENT OF LIFT by Melinda Gates © 2019 by Melinda Gates, reprinted by permission of Flatiron Books, a division of Macmillan Publishing Group, LLC, All rights reserved, 2–3.

3. *Mass Shootings in America 2009-2019*, accessed December 23, 2020, https://maps.everytownresearch.org/massshootingsreports/mass-shootings -in-america-2009-2019.

4. Thomson Reuters Foundation Annual Poll, *The World's Most Dangerous Countries For Women, 2018*, https://poll2018.trust.org.

5. Jimmy Carter, "Women Live in a Profoundly Different, More Dangerous World," Thomson Reuters Foundation News, November 25, 2013, https://theelders.org/news/women-live-profoundly-different-more- dangerous-world.

Chapter 1 Life's Hard Knocks

1.	Laura Bates, *Everyday Sexism* (U.K., Simon & Schuster, 2015), 21.

Chapter 2 The Place to Begin

1.	Sam Killermann, "It's Pronounced Metrosexual," http://www.itspronounced metrosexual.com/about/.

2.	Betty Friedan, *The Feminine Mystique* (U.S., W.W. Norton, 1963).

3.	Frank Pittman, *Man Enough* (New York: Penguin, 1993), xiii.

4.	Patrick Rafferty, "Former NFL Player Joe Ehrmann Speaks," *The Daily Iowan*, accessed December 8, 2020, https://dailyiowan.com/2009/06/26/former-nfl-player-joe-ehrmann-speaks/.

5.	Graeme Green, "A Word with Gloria Steinem," New Internationalist, July 5, 2017, https://newint.org/columns/finally/2016/05/01/interview-gloria-steinem, reprinted by kind permission of New Internationalist, Copyright New Internationalist, https://newint.org.

6.	Jeffrey Marx, "He Turns Boys Into Men," August 29, 2004, https://www.ipce.info/library_3/files/coach.htm.

Chapter 3 A Lesson from History

1.	"Abigail and John Adams Converse on Women's Rights, 1776," *The American Yawp Reader*, accessed December 12, 2020, https://www.americanyawp.com/reader/the-american-revolution/abigail-and-john-adams-converse-on-womens-rights-1776/.

2.	Ibid.

3.	"RUTH SAYS: MAKE WOMEN A PART OF THE CONSTITUTION! and She's Still at It . . ." *SheVille*, September 24, 2020, https://sheville.org/era-bulletin-board-ratify-equal-rights-amendment-now/.

4.   "All-American Girls Professional Baseball League," *Encyclopedia Britannica, Inc.*, accessed November 26, 2020, https://www.britannica.com/topic/All-American-Girls-Professional -Baseball-League.

5.   Susan King, "National Film Registry Selects 25 Films for Preservation," *Los Angeles Times*, Dec. 19, 2012.

6.   Julie DiCaro, "Ugly Truth about Women in Sports and Social Media," *SI.com*, last modified September 27, http://www.si.com/cauldron/2015/09/27/ twitter-threats-vile-remarks-women-sports-journalists.

7.   Ibid.

8.   Ibid.

9.   Alexa Keyes, "Rush Limbaugh Doubles Down on Sandra Fluke, Offering 'As Much Aspirin to Put Between Her Knees as She Wants'," *ABC News*, (blog), March 2, 2012, http://abcnews.go.com/blogs/politics/2012/03/ rush-limbaugh-sandra-fluke-a-slut-and-prostitute/.

10. Friedan, *The Feminine Mystique*, 1963.

11. Debra Michals, "Shirley Chisholm," *National Women's History Museum*, last modified December 27, 2020, http://www.womenshistory.org/ education-resources/biographies/shirley-chisholm.

12. Stephanie Townrow, "Rosa Parks Refuses to Move: On this Day, December 1," *Gilder Lehrman Institute of American History*, last modified November 26, 2020, https://www.gilderlehrman.org/news/ rosa-parks-refuses-move-day-december-1.

13. National Women's History Museum (NWHM), https://www.women- shistory.org/education-resources/biographies/fannie-lou-hamer.

14. Debra Michals, "Sojourner Truth," *National Women's History Museum*, last modified 2015, http://www.womenshistory.org/education-resources/ biographies/sojourner-truth.

15.   Hardie Grant Books, *Pocket RBG Wisdom: Supreme Quotes and Inspired Musings from Ruth Bader Ginsburg*, London: Hardie Grant Books, 2019, 46–47.

16.   Ibid, 87.

Chapter 4 The Facts Aren't Pretty: Nevertheless We Persist!

1.   Why, In 2020, There Are Still 260m Children Out of School, *Their World*, https://theirworld.org/news/20-reasons-why-260m -children-are-out-of-school-in-2020

2.   "Two-Thirds of the World's Illiterate Adults Are Women, U.N. Says," *Education World*, http://www.educationworld.com/a_news/ two-thirds-worlds-illiterate-adults-are-women-un-says-486650943.

3.   "10 Reasons Why Investing in Women and Girls Is so Important," *Global Citizen*, accessed February 12, 2021, https://www.globalcitizen.org/en/ content/10-reasons-why-investing-in-women-and-girls-is-so/.

4.   "Why the Majority of the World's Poor Are Women," *Oxfam International*, January 20, 2020, https://www.oxfam.org/en/why-majority-worlds -poor-are-women.

5.   Ibid.

6.   "The Impact of Equal Pay On Poverty and the Economy," *Institute for Women's Policy Research*, September 6, 2020, https://iwpr.org/iwpr- publications/briefing-paper/the-impact-of-equal-pay-on-poverty-and -the-economy/.

7.   Ibid.

8.   Alanna Vagianos, "30 Shocking Domestic Violence Statistics That Remind Us It's an Epidemic," *HuffPost*, December 7, 2017, http://www.huffpost.com/entry/domestic-violence-statistics_n _5959776.

9. "11 Facts About Domestic and Dating Violence," *DoSomething.org*, http://www.dosomething.org/us/facts/11-facts-about-domestic-and-dating-violence.

10. Ibid.

11. Ibid.

12. Rebecca Solnit, "A Rape a Minute, a Thousand Corpses a Year," *The Nation*, last modified June 29, 2015, http://www.thenation.com/article/rape-minute-thousand-corpses-year/.

13. "Black Woman and Domestic Violence," *Blackburn Center*, https://www.blackburncenter.org/post/2020/02/26/black-women-domestic-violence.

14. Alanna Vagianos, "30 Shocking Domestic Violence Statistics That Remind Us It's an Epidemic," http://www.huffpost.com/entry/domestic-violence-statistics_n_5959776. (accessed November 20, 2020).

15. Ibid.

16. Ibid.

17. "Campus Sexual Violence: Statistics," *RAINN*, http://www.rainn.org/statistics/campus-sexual-violence.

18. "U.S. Military Men Sexually Assault One-Third of Fellow Female Soldiers," *CODEPINK*, http://www.codepink.org/u_s_military_men_sexually_assault_one_third_ of_fellow_female_soldiers.

19. "Victims of Sexual Violence: Statistics," RAINN, accessed November 28, 2020, https://www.rainn.org/statistics/victims-sexual-violence.

20. Rebecca Solnit, "A Rape a Minute, a Thousand Corpses a Year," http:/www.thenation.com/article/rape-minute-thousand-corpses-year/.

21. "Female Genital Mutilation," *World Health Organization*, last modified January 31, 2018, http://www.who.int/news-room/fact-sheets/detail/female-genital-mutilation.

22. "The Facts on Child Marriage," *International Women's Health Coalition*, http://www.iwhc.org/resources/facts-child-marriage/.

23. Ibid.

24. "40 Million in Modern Slavery and 152 Million in Child Labour Around the World," *International Labour Organization*, September 19, 2017, http://www.ilo.org/global/about-the-ilo/newsroom/news/WCMS_574717/lang--en/index.htm.

25. "11 Facts about Human Trafficking," *DoSomething.org*, http://www.dosome-thing.org/us/facts/11-facts-about-human-trafficking.

26. "The Facts," *Polaris*, last modified November 9, 2018, http://www.polarisproject.org/human-trafficking/facts.

27. Tanya Tarr, "How This Study Misses the Mark on Equal Pay and the Pay Gap," *Forbes*, last modified November 30, 2018, http://www.forbes.com/sites/tanyatarr/2018/11/30/how-this-study-misses-the-mark-on-equal-pay-and-the-pay-gap/#5c69a35b42c1.

28. Chris Wilson, "Equal Pay Day: How Much Women Lose Over a Lifetime," *Time*, last modified April 2, 2019, http://www.time.com/5562269/equal-pay-day -women-men-lifetime-wages/.

29. Claire Zillman, "The Fortune 500 Has More Female CEOs Than Ever Before," *Fortune*, last modifed May 16, 2019, http://www.fortune.com/2019/05/16/ fortune-500-female-ceos/.

30. "Women in Elective Office 2019," *Center for American Women and Politics (CAWP)*, last modified August 29, 2019, http://www.cawp.rutgers.edu/women-elective-office-2019.

31. "2018, Women and Political Leadership—Female Heads of State and Heads of Government," *Women in International Politics*, last modified March 26, 2018, http://firstladies.international/2018/02/20/2018-women- and-political-leadership-female-heads-of-state-and-heads-of -government/.

32. United Nations Fourth World Conference on Women, accessed December 14, 2020, https://www.un.org/esa/gopher-data/conf/fwcw/conf/gov/950905175653.txt.

33. *The Global Gender Gap Report 2018,* World Economic Forum, last modified 2018, http://www3.weforum.org/docs/WEF_GGGR_2018.pdf.

34. Ibid.

35. Jamille Bigio, "When Women Are at the Negotiating Table, Peace Lasts Longer," *Apolitical,* last modified November 21, 2017, http://www.apolitical.co/solution_article/ women-negotiating-table-peace -lasts-longer/.

36. "Women Hold the Key to Building a World Free from Hunger and Poverty," *Food and Agriculture Organization of the United Nations,* http://www.fao.org/news/story/en/item/460267/icode/.

37. Jackson Katz, "Violence against Women—It's a Men's Issue," *TED,* http://www.ted.com/talks/jackson_katz_violence_against_women_it_s_a _men_s_issue.

38. Zaron Burnett III, "A Gentleman's Guide to Rape Culture," *HuffPost,* last modified August 5, 2014, http://www.huffpost.com/entry/ guide-to-rape-culture_b_5440553.

39. Zaron Burnett III, "A Gentleman's Guide to the #MeToo Era," *Medium,* last modified July 24, 2018, http://www.medium.com/s/man-interrupted/ https-medium-com-zaron3-guide-to-being-a-gentleman-in-the-metoo-era-f87ef12a9caa.

40. *The Representation Project,* http://www.therepresentationproject.org/ about-us/.

41. "Gloria Steinem: 10 Quotes from the Front-Lines of the Fight for Equality," *Equality Now,* accessed December 25, 2020, https://www.equalitynow.org/gloria_steinem_quotes.

Chapter 5 *Oh*, the Stories We Tell

1. Jan Morris, *Conundrum* (Faber & Faber, 2011), 166.

2. "2018 TIMPANI Toy Study," *Eastern Connecticut State*, http://www.easternct.edu/cece/timpani/.

3. David Miller Sadker, Karen Zittleman, Myra Sadker, *Still Failing at Fairness: How Gender Bias Cheats Girls and Boys in School and What We Can Do about It* (Scribner, 2009).

4. Gerda Lerner, *The Creation of Patriarchy, Gerda Lerner—Oxford University Press*, Oxford University Press, http://www.global.oup.com/academic/product/the-creation-of-patriarchy-9780195051858. vii.

5. Emily Dwass, "A Biblical Woman's Tale That Won Readers' Hearts," *Los Angeles Times*, April 24, 2000, https://www.latimes.com/archives/la-xpm-2000-apr-24-cl-22773-story.html.

6. "Bechdel Test Movie List," http://www.bechdeltest.com/.

7. Cordelia Fine, *Delusions of Gender: How Our Minds, Society, and Neurosexism Create Difference* (W.W. Norton & Co., 2011).

8. Fine, *Delusions of Gender*, xviii.

9. Fine, *Delusions of Gender*, xix.

10. Fine, *Delusions of Gender*, 8.

11. Fine, *Delusions of Gender*, 9.

12. Gina Rippon, "How 'Neurosexism' Is Holding Back Gender Equality—and Science Itself," *The Conversation*, last modified May 14, 2019, http://www.theconversation.com/how-neurosexism-is-holding-back-gender-equality-and-science-itself-67597.

13. John Timmer, "Gender Gap in Spatial Abilities Depends on Females' Role in Society," *Ars Technica*, last modified August 30, 2011, http://www.arstechnica.com/science/2011/08/gender-gap-in-spatial-reasoning-mia-in-matrilineal-society/.

14. "Yes, 'Mind of Oppressed' Quote by South Africa's Steve Biko," Africa Check, accessed December 15, 2020, https://africacheck.org/fbcheck/yes-mind-of-oppressed-quote-by-south-africas-steve-biko/.

Chapter 6 The Shift: From Habits of Inequality to Habits of Equality

1. E.C. Schneider, D.O. Sarnak, D. Squires, A. Shah, M. M. Doty, *Mirror, Mirror 2017: International Comparison Reflects Flaws and Opportunities for Better U.S. Health Care* (The Commonwealth Fund, July 2017).

2. Ibid.

3. *Report: The Bottom Line: Connecting Corporate Performance and Gender Diversity,* Catalyst, last modified January 15, 2004, http://www.catalyst.org/research/the-bottom-line-connecting-corporate-performance-and-gender-diversity/.

4. Marcus Noland, Tyler Moran, "Study: Firms with More Women in the C-suite Are More Profitable," *Harvard Business Review*, last modified February 8, 2016, http://www.hbr.org/2016/02/study-firms-with-more-women-in-the-c-suite-are-more-profitable.

5. "The Corporate Leaders of Gender Diversity in the Boardroom and Executive Suite," *UC Davis*, http://www.gsm.ucdavis.edu/sites/main/files/file-attachments/ ucdaviswomenstudy2015_top25.pdf.

6. Sarah Kliff, "The Research Is Clear: Electing More Women Changes How Government Works," *Vox*, last modified March 8, 2017, http://www.vox.com/2016/7/27/12266378/electing-women-congress-hillary-clinton?f bclid=IwAR0t5IowXyL3BiadtGe4CDaysVGL4oQLMOFFCe4w5Swr N2NyBHTK-WrC0lQ.

7. Alice Park, "Researchers Find Women Make Better Surgeons Than Men," *Time*, last modified October 10, 2017, http://www.time.com/4975232/women-surgeon-surgery/.

8.   Jamilie Bigio, "When Women Are at the Negotiating Table, Peace Lasts Longer," https://apolitical.co/en/solution_article/women-negotiating-table-peace-lasts-longer.

9.   "Facts and Figures: Peace and Security," *U.N. Women*, http://www.unwomen.org/en/what-we-do/peace-and-security/facts-and-figures.

10.   Michael Schneider, "A Google Study Revealed That the Best Managers Use Emotional Intelligence And Share This 1 Trait," *Inc.com*, last modified November 16, 2017, http://www.inc.com/michael-schneider/a-google-study-revealed-that-best-managers-use-emotional-intelligence-share-this-1-trait.html.

11.   "*Full Report: The State of Gender Equality for U.S. Adolescents,*" Sept 10, 2018, Plan USA, accessed December 25, 2020, https://www.planusa.org/full-report-the-state-of-gender-equality-for-us-adolescents.

12.   Gerda Lerner, *The Creation of Patriarchy*, New York: Oxford University Press, 1986, 232.

13.   Martin Luther King Jr., and Coretta Scott King, *The Words of Martin Luther King Jr.* (HarperCollins Publishers, 2014),16.

14.   Lerner, The Creation of Patriarchy, 232.

15.   Jessie Mooney DiGiovanna, "Who Traditionally Pays for the Wedding?" *Brides*, last modified September 3, 2017, http://www.brides.com/story/what-your-family-pays-for-wedding-planning.

16.   Liz Susong, "How Do We Choose a Last Name as a Same-sex Married Couple?" *Brides*, last modifed July 27, 2017, http://www.brides.com/story/dispatches-from-a-feminist-bride-same-sex-last-names.

17.   Karen Mansfield, "What's in a Name? More Women Keeping Maiden Names after Marriage," *Observer*, March 26, 2018, https://observer-reporter.com/news/localnews/whats-in-a-name-more-women-keeping-maiden-names-after-marriage/article_10036908-173e-11e8-be34-9b8a2ac73f79.html.

18. Lerner, *The Creation of Patriarchy*, 234.

19. Motoko Rich, "Japan's Working Mothers: Record Responsibilities, Little Help from Dads," *New York Times*, last modifed February 2, 2019, http://www.nytimes.com/2019/02/02/world/asia/japan-working -mothers.html.

20. Emma Anderson, "Women Do 60 Percent More Unpaid Work Than Men: Report," *The Local*, last modifed April 24, 2017, http://www. thelocal.de/20170424/ women-do-60-percent-more-unpaid-work-than -men-report.

21. "Men Increase Their Share of Unpaid Housework," *Statistiska Centralbyrån*, last modified August 31, 2011, http://www.scb.se/en/find- ing-statistics/statistics-by-subject-area/living-conditions/living-conditions/ the-swedish-time-use-survey/pong/statistical-news/the-swedish-time-use -survey-2010/.

22. Kelley Holland, "Division of Labor: Same-sex Couples More Likely to Share Chores, Study Says," *NBCNews.com*, last modified June 11, 2015, http://www.nbcnews.com/business/consumer/division-labor-same-sex -couples-more-likely-share-chores-study-n369921.

23. Fine, *Delusions of Gender*, 85.

24. *"The Geena Benchmark Report: 2007–2017,"* See Jane, http://see- jane.org/research-informs-empowers/the-geena-benchmark-report -2007-2017/.

25. *2018-2019 Where We Are on TV*, GLAAD Media Institute, https://glaad. org/files/WWAT/WWAT_GLAAD_2018-2019.pdf.

26. *"Full Report: The State of Gender Equality for U.S. Adolescents,"* Sept 10, 2018, Plan USA, accessed December 25, 2020, https:// www.planusa.org/full-report-the-state-of-gender-equality-for -us-adolescents.

Chapter 7 The Circle of Life

1. Joe Ehrmann, "The Three Scariest Words a Boy Will Ever Hear," *Voice Male magazine*, October 13, 2015, https://voicemalemagazine.org/the-three-scariest-words-a-boy-will-ever-hear/.

Chapter 8 The Seven Habits of Equality That Will Change the World

1. "WOMEN ARE NOT PROTECTED in the U. S. Constitution—Here Are the Ramifications," *SheVille*, October 8, 2020, https://sheville.org/1ramifications-of-women-not-being-included-in-the-u-s-constitution/.

2. *The Global Gender Gap Report 2018*, World Economic Forum, https://www.weforum.org/reports/the-global-gender-gap-report-2018.

3. *Global Peace Index 2018: Measuring Peace in a Complex World*, Institute for Economics & Peace, last modified June 2018, http://visionofhumanity.org/reports.

4. *The Global Gender Gap Report 2018*, World Economic Forum, https://www.weforum.org/reports/the-global-gender-gap-report-2018.

5. *World Happiness Report 2019*, March 20, 2019, https://worldhappiness.report/ed/2019/.

6. *2018 Environmental Performance Index*, Yale Center for Environmental Law & Policy, Yale University in collaboration with the World Economic Forum (Center for International Earth Science Information Network, Columbia University), https://epi.yale.edudownloadsepi2018reportv06191901.pdf.

7. *The Legatum Prosperity Index™ 2019: Creating the Pathways from Poverty to Prosperity*, Legatum Institute, https://li.com/reports/2019-legatum-prosperity-index/.

8. Marcus Noland and Tyler Moran, "Study: Firms with More Women in the C-Suite Are More Profitable," *Harvard Business Review*, February 8, 2016, https://hbr.org/2016/02/study-firms-with-more-women-in-the-c-suite-are-more-profitable.

9. Lynn Taliento, and Madgavkar Anu, "Power with Purpose: How Women's Leadership Boosts the Economy and Society," *Devex*, March 7, 2016, https://www.devex.com/news/power-with-purpose-how-women-s-leadership-boosts-the-economy-and-society-87845. (accessed November 29, 2020).

10. *The World's Most Dangerous Countries For Women 2018*, Thomson Reuters Foundation, https://poll2018.trust.org.

11. HeartMath is a registered trademark of Quantum Intech, Inc.

12. Jacob Koffler, "Maiden Names: Here Are Places Women Can't Take Their Husband's Name," *Time*, Last modified June 29, 2015, http://www.time.com/3940094/maiden-married-names-countries/.

Chapter 9 Voices of the Future

1. Marjorie Julian Spruill, *Divided We Stand: The Battle Over Women's Rights and Family Values That Polarized American Politics* (Bloomsbury, 2018).

2. "5 Ways Education Can Help End Extreme Poverty," *Global Partnership for Education*, last modified October 17, 2016, http://www.globalpartnership.org/blog/5-ways-education-can-help-end-extreme-poverty.

3. "Women Hold the Key to Building a World Free from Hunger and Poverty," *FAO*, last modified December 16, 2016, http://www.fao.org/news/story/en/item /460267/icode/.

4. Joe McCarthy, "Educating Girls Is the Key to Ending Poverty," *Global Citizen*, last modified August 7, 2015, http://www.globalcitizen.org/en/content/educating-girls-is-the-key-to-ending-poverty.

5. Soraya Chemaly, "Why Everyday Gender Inequality Could Lead to Our Next War," *Women's Media Center*, last modified September 14, 2014, http://www.womens mediacenter.com/women-under-siege/why-everyday-gender-inequality-could-lead-to-our-next-war.

6.   "Gender Equality Crucial to Tackling Climate Change—U.N.,"
     UNFCCC, last modified February 19, 2018, http://unfccc.int/news/
     gender-equality-crucial-to-tackling-climate-change-un.

7.   "Gender and Climate Change," *IUCN*, last modified December 5,
     2018, http://www.iucn.org/resources/issues-briefs/gender-and
     -climate-change.

About the Author

Laurie Levin has moved from corporate executive to mother, transformation coach, and author, always a feminist and social justice advocate, always hopeful. She hopes *Call Me a Woman: On Our Way to Equality and Peace* contributes to the happiness and well-being of every person on the planet, transforming life as we know it.

Levin lives near the ocean, one of her greatest sources of peace and tranquility. #healthyhappyequal www.laurielevin.online

Made in the USA
Middletown, DE
27 January 2023

23258186R00132